Hell
On
Wheels

Hell on Wheels

a tour stories compilation

Greg Jacobs

rockpress publishing
p.o.b. 99090 san diego ca 92169 usa

©1994 Rockpress Publishing.
ISBN 0-9627013-3-5
Library of Congress Catalog # 92-060980

Opinions expressed herein are the views of the individual
interviewees and do not necessarily reflect the views of the
author or publisher. Basically, this is what the bands told us,
so if you have a problem with it, talk to them.

Thank you: (In no particular order, except the first one):
Linda Jacobs (Greg's Mom), all the bands that participated,
Gary Hustwit, Christian Hoffman, Felicia Crossley, Alma
Kirchner, T. Racey Groce, Amy Seidenwurm, Jeff Abarta, Kim
White, Max Burgos, Angie Martin, Bobbi Gayle, Karen
Lindstrom, Scott Parker, Pleasant Gehman, Liz Garo, Melanie
Tusquellas, and everyone we forgot.

Covers and book design by Gary Hustwit
Cover photos by John Lee (van) and Ted Drake (guitar)
Edited (sort of) by Christian Hoffman and Gary Hustwit

Printed in the U.S.A.

Contents

Intro

The idea of compiling *Hell On Wheels* actually came from my Mom. Gary (publisher) asked me if I had any ideas and if I wanted to write a book. I was an Art major in college, not a Literature major. So, writing a book was one of the last things on my mind. I mentioned the book thing one day while talking to my mom on the phone and she said "Why don't you write a book full of tour stories. You always had so much fun hearing and retelling the stories you heard from Big Drill Car when they got home from tour." Well, I pitched the idea to Gary and we were off, kind of. I mean the interviews were fun to do; it's fun hearing the stories. But then you have to transcribe them. Plus I have a real job that keeps me very busy. What I'm trying to say is, I lagged! But, I think these stories are great, it doesn't matter if they were told to me yesterday or two years ago.

– Greg

ALL

"...man, a lot of fags were coming up to me. And they were like, touching me and stuff..."

ALL

Interviewed by Greg Jacobs in their bus outside
SOMA, San Diego, CA. Present were Bug Phace
(roadie) and Scott Reynolds (vocals).

Bug: Hey Scotty. Where was the show in Germany
where, uh, I sicked a fag on you?

Scott: Oooooh dude!

Bug: What was the name of that place?

Scott: I don't know, I can't remember. But that
sucked!

Bug: Someone else will know, I'll ask 'em. But, uh, I
was sitting there doing merch (selling t-shirts) and
a lot, man, a lot of fags were coming up to me. And
they were like, touching me and stuff. And this
guy, a big guy too, totally decked in leather head
to toe, red leather, sits down next to me....

Greg: Was he your type, Scott?

Scott: This ain't a funny story!

Bug: Sits down next to me and puts his hand on my
leg and says (something indecipherable in German) and he's all loaded drunk. And I go, "get, get
away man, I don't speak any German! Leave me
alone!" And he's like bigger than Jim is, man.

Jim: He was probably telling you in German how
he wants to fuck you!

Bug: He was! He was a fucking fag! And, like, he
goes to put his hand on my leg again and I'm all,
dude leave me alone. And I pushed him away. And
he was big, man, he had 150 pounds on me, easy!
Fuck, so I see Scott walking by, and I'm just think-

ing, "I wish someone would fucking relieve me (from the t-shirt booth). Someone's gotta come by and take over." I see Scott and I'm all, "Hey Scott will you watch the booth for a minute?" Scott sits down and I take off, I go, "Yeah, I'll be right back."

So I split man, I had to cool out for a second, cause it kinda made me a little nervous, man. I was kinda scared. He was big! You know! So, Scott's sitting down and I'm sitting in the dressing room peaking around the corner and Scott's, like, pushing him off. And he sees me looking and he knows (what I did) and he just goes," What a dick! He left me and he knew!" I didn't tell him or nothing. So, fucking our road manager, Whoopi, our German road manger. And Scott just goes, "Get this guy out of the club, man!" And Whoopi goes off on him, gets the security. So I'm back in the dressing room, and there are these two doors that open (like a western saloon), I'm standing there talking to Bill and the two doors just go BAM! (fly open) And he's (Scott) bright red! His neck's like a cobra, man! He just picks me up against the wall and he's all, " Ahhhhhhhhh!" Freaking out man! And Bill was just shitting! It was hilarious! Cos I looked around the corner and the little fag's got his hand on Scott's leg.......

aMINIATURE

"The smell,
however, was
still there,
no matter how
hard we tried
to ignore it."

aMINIATURE

As told by Christian Hoffman (drummer).

John Lee was doing about 75 miles per hour in our
Ford Club Wagon, tearing up the Ohio Express-
ways. He was really annoyed, going that fast,
trying to keep up with the van we were following.
We were touring with another band and they had a
rental; they could care less what happened to it.
We had just bought our van three days before and
had driven straight from San Diego to Cincinati for
our first show. Yeah, we're an eager little bunch.

From Cincinati we were headed to Toronto, so we
were in a bit of a rush, but not that rushed. I was
sitting shotgun, Colin and Pippin (from Inch) were
behind us on a bench seat and Kevin was on the
back bench. Colin, being the dexterous fellow that
he is, threw a cigarette out one window and it flew
back in another. He was too embarassed to admit
his mistake until John asked me, "Do you smell
something burning?" "Actually, I do John," I answered. Colin went back to find his burning butt.

This is where the tension begins to rise. John, who
is especially sensitive to the inner workings of
machinery, noticed that the aroma was slightly
different than that of tobacco or paper. I was
becoming increasingly nervous, as was the rest of
the gang. Colin then yells, "I found it!" and throws
the butt out the window. The smell, however, was
still there, no matter how hard we tried to ignore
it. Thirty seconds or so passed before John and I
gave each other that "SOMETHING IS VERY WRONG
HERE" look.

Not ten seconds after "the look," the van seemed to drop out from underneath me with a horrible crash. Remember we are doing about 75 mph here. There is immediate disorientation. We all blurt out intelligent (but appropriate) comments like, "FUCK" or "SHIT" Colin yells, "Hey! There goes our tire!" It was bouncing down the road. Pippin is repeatedly screaming, "Don't step on the brakes!!!" And I am staring at John as he calmly answers Pippin with an "I know," and guides that hunk of skidding steel to a halt on the side of the freeway, about a half mile from where the tire fell off, and just in front of a rest area in Nowhere, Ohio. The first words out of John's mouth after we stopped were, "The van hasn't driven that straight the entire trip." People seem to deal with peculiar situations in peculiar ways.

The entire wheel had fallen off of the axel: tire; rim; everything. The tow truck driver said that the wheel was only being held on by a brake cable for the last few miles. He also said that if John had hit the brakes we probably would have spun out and went rolling into the gully next to the freeway. We would have been dead, smashed by our own instruments.

We spent three days in Findlay, Ohio, did one show, and were blessed with an angel of mercy by the name of Dean, who was the driver for Wrecker Bear Towing. He charged us virtually nothing, after driving all over that part of the state on a holiday looking for the parts and then repairing the wheel of our van, by himself.

Babes in Toyland

"...basically all I could think about at this point was, "Goddamnit, the Russians are here!"

BABES IN TOYLAND

Lori from Babes in Toyland talked to the ever-lovely Angie Martin in Minneapolis.

Lori: The first story...which one should I tell?

Angie: Give us a couple.

Lori: The earthquake or the accident?

Angie: I think the earthquake.

Lori: Well the earthquake was the big earthquake that happened in San Francisco. When was that, in October of 1990? We were supposed to play in San Francisco that night, we had the night off before that. I, of course, drank about a whole bottle of Jaegermeister. I had a terrible hangover. We were staying at a friends house right on Market and Church there in San Francisco. Michelle needed a ride somewhere on Upper Haight. So I gave her a ride, and I was completely hung over. I took her up there and I ran into Tom Arnold, who is now married to Roseanne Barr.

Angie: You just saw him on the street?

Lori: Yeah I know him, because when he used to live in Minneapolis we would go bowling all the time on Sunday nights. He, and Maggie the pro-moter for the Uptown Club, and Liz Wednesday, who is a comedian now, and me. So I ran into him, and he introduced me to Roseanne, and they were going to go to the World Series that night. We went for a drink and stuff, and then I went back down to the apartment on Market, because I had to take a nap before I played that night. I was yawning, I was thinking that I would not be able to even breath that night at the show.

So I drive back down there, I'd say its between 2:30 and 4:00 in the afternoon, I don't even know for sure. I parked the car and was going into the apartment, and there was this guy putting up these posters that said "The Russians are coming! The Russians are coming!" I'm reading it and it says "on earth and on sea," it was some political thing. I just remember seeing that and I was just like "arrgh." I went into the apartment, went to the room where I was sleeping, laid down on the bed, and went to sleep.

I was in a dead sleep, and all of a sudden there was this "BOOM!!!." And I was like thrown out of my bed. You know that feeling when your kind of still drunk, hung over? I was like "What the Hell!!?" I didn't know where I was! I didn't know who I was! I didn't know what was going on. I looked in the bed to see if someone had pushed me out. I didn't go to bed with anybody. I was really con- fused. I was like, "What am I doing!?" Everything started shaking and moving and all the wood started cracking in the corners. Everything was falling off the mantle over the fireplace. I started running up and down the hallway, there is a long hallway with a front door and a back door. And basically at this point all I could think about was, "Goddamnit the Russians are here!!!" I am running up and down the hallway in my boxer shorts and a tank top thinking, "Are they going to come in the front door or the back door?" I was so confused. All of a sudden I was like, "Wait a minute. I'm in San Francisco. It's a fucking earthquake. Duh!"

So I opened up the front door, and the street was literally in waves, like waves on the water. It was like the epicenter, just because Market street was

where the main tremble was. And it was amazing!
I had never experienced anything like that! And of
course, obviously, we didn't play that night. Everything was destroyed. It was unbelievable. Cat was
on the ocean so she really didn't know what was
going on. She didn't even know what had happened because she was on the ocean with somebody. She really missed out, and Michelle was
having coffee up on the Upper Haight. She kind of
felt it but it was nothing like where I was. And it
was really weird because my body was really
effected. I was still really tired but I couldn't sleep
for two days. Mentally I was like, weird, kinda'
cool. I experienced that. That was amazing you
know? It was sad and all at the same time, what
happened to all those people and stuff.

So being the entrepreneur that I was, I'm not really
a capitalist or anything but, knowing that I was
broke and not going to be playing any shows for
the next couple of days, I went out at like 5:00 in
the morning. I went down to 16th and Valencia in
the Mission where I have a friend who has a news-
paper stand. They had the two different papers,
the Chronicle and the San Francisco Examiner, and
because all the electricity and all the power was
out they did them on the old hand machines. So
they made both papers off the original press. I had
about fifteen dollars on me, each paper was, I don't
know, 50 cents or something. I spent all my money
and bought an equal amount of each. There were
only like two-thousand copies total made of each, it
wasn't very many. And I bought as many as I
could. So later on in the day everybody was ram-
bling for a paper. I was like, "Two dollars each!
Two dollars each!" I sold them (snap) like that. I
wish I had a million more. I kept a couple for

myself.

I was like, I'm going to make some money! Because
I was poor, and all these business men were like,
"Ahh, fuck you!" And I said, "Fuck you! Give me
two dollars for them. You want one?" You're
wearing a five million dollar suit. Whatever, I sold
them all and ended up having some money to live
off. I guess it was kind of a scam thing but I don't
care.

Angie: Was your van, or whatever you were travel-
ling in okay?

Lori: Yeah it was okay, and actually I sat in the van
and turned on the radio because none of the electricity worked, but the car stereo did. There were
people all over the place standing around my van,
listening to all the news. It was really amazing,
and the World Series was going on and I was
thinking, "Oh my God! It was probably Roseanne
and Tom Arnold having sex!"

And because we didn't play that night, the next
night we played a benefit for earthquake victims at
the Kennel Club, with Fetchin' Bones and a couple
of other bands. We got some money for the people
whose houses burnt down, and to get some food on
the shelves.

And the really weird thing was that the next time
we were in town, I was like, "You better hold on to
yourselves cause there are going to be some earthquakes!" And that night there were two small
earthquakes again!

The other story, I seem to think that it happened on
the same tour. It was Friday the 23rd, we were
driving looking for Superstition Highway, and it
was myself, Cat, Michelle and Dave our soundman.
I was driving, Cat was in the passenger seat,

Michelle was sleeping on the loft, and Dave was asleep on the floor, we had bean bags down there. We are in Arizona, looking for Superstition Highway in Phoenix. I'm driving along thinking about how we have been completely ripped off, our van completely cleaned out in New York. We've been in hurricanes, earthquakes, tornados in Kansas. We had to stay in because, there were tornados all over the place and our car had broken down.

The thing that I was thinking about was, my friend is Robert Williams the artist. He's pretty cool, basically all of his paintings have one huge story in them. I had gone out to his house when I was out in L.A. He had invited me out there and we were sitting around chatting. He had brought up that maybe he could do a record cover for us sometime because he is really into the band, and he is also a friend of mine. So I'm driving along and I'm thinking, well, he could do our next record cover. And I had this idea that it would be this picture, he kinda' does cartoon realistic weird stuff, of the Babes in Toyland driving along in a van, then having all these different scenarios around us. It would tell the story of all the different things that have happened to us with God up in the clouds with a pair of dice in his hands. And on each side of the dice it says, tornado, earthquake, storms, blizzards, hurricanes, we were in a hurricane out in South Carolina. We were supposed to play there and the venue blew down the day before so it was cancelled. So I'm thinking of God standing up there with a big pair of dice ready to roll them to see what was in store for the Babes on tour. I had the whole thing in my head, and I thought, you know, the only thing we haven't been in is a car accident.

So I'm thinking that as I look across and I see this pickup truck with a camper on it, and all of a sudden the rear tire comes off of it and goes into the ditch between the lanes. It was a two lane highway and the truck had been coming toward us. For a second I thought I was daydreaming because of what I had just been thinking about.

I see this tire come off of the pickup truck, which is probably doing about sixty-five miles per hour, and goes into the ditch. It starts to pick up tons of speed, it went down into this gully and then starts to come up the other side. It flies through the air and I'm looking at it and I'm like, "Oh my fucking God!!!" I screamed and I yell, "Cat!!" I think she might have been sleeping sitting up. I slammed on the brakes, Michelle flies out of the loft, lands on top of Dave. There is no one else around us. This tire storms straight at us, fucking smashes...just totals our van. It smashes the windshield, tears the roof off the van, and then goes bouncing and rolls a mile into the desert. It was amazing, I was sitting there thinking, "Oh my God!"

Cat and I both had sunglasses on, thank God because we would be blind. We were sheathed with glass. Cat got it worse than me because of the angle that it came it got her more, but if I would not have yelled...She kind of ducked down so it got her more in the legs and a little right around her chin. She has no scars, just one little one on her leg. But she was really bloody because of all the glass and we used the picture for our Australian 45 with Handsome and Gretel and Pearl. One side of the cover is a picture I took of Cat in the back of the police car. I had immediately gotten my polaroid and took a picture of her. It was amazing. She was wearing a red dress with a red bow in her hair, and there was all this blood and the cop is standing there. It looked like it was totally staged. The cops were really cool. It was just weird. The first thing I did was get out of the truck and I was just crying, not because of the van...I mean I was scared because of what had happened, but I knew everyone was okay. I was just freaked because it was exactly what I was thinking about. Its Friday the 23rd, we're looking for Superstition Highway, we've never been in an accident, and this tire goes flying through the air, totals our van.

The truck that lost the tire kept going. The cops go chasing down looking for him. They get him. He is a forty-five year old Mexican man who didn't have his license. It was his mother's truck. And he only had one eye.

Yes, he only had one eye. The other socket was completely empty and he didn't wear an eye patch or anything. He was a one-eyed Mexican that lived with his mom. And he just kept driving. They found him like two and a half miles down the road, driving with three wheels, trying to get away because he was in so much trouble. And this is only the beginning of the goddamn story.

They tow the truck away. I did know one woman in the area who had lived downstairs from me in Minneapolis. She lived in Phoenix and I tried to call her. We all went to the hospital. They pulled the glass out of Cat, I had a little glass, it was nothing major. But if we hadn't been wearing sunglasses, I mean there was glass just sheathed into the sunglasses.

So Heidi finally gets a hold of us. She comes and gets us and we stay at her house for about three days. We are looking for a van. We are in trouble. We have this tour to do, we have to find a van and we are stuck in Phoenix, Arizona. So we go and rent one from Rent-A-Wreck, and the woman who rented us one, her name was Amy. She was a nice, kind of heavy woman, she just worked in this place. So we rent this '75 Ford van. We did not like it and did not want to buy it but we had been running around and all the vans we saw were either way too expensive or they were just shitty vans. We just kept looking everyday from sunrise to sunset and we couldn't find anything. So we thought, "what about this van we are using now?"

I called up this woman Amy at the Rent-A-Wreck, kind of late at night. She answered the phone and I asked, "What do you think about us buying the van? Is that possible?" And she says, "Well, I'll have to talk to the owner about it, but she's not here right now. She's here everyday but she left for the night. If you want to call tomorrow, she comes in about 12:00 to 1:00 in the afternoon." I said okay and hung up.

The next day we're driving around and I decide to call her. Its about 1:00 in the afternoon, I say, "Amy?"

And she says "Yeah?"

I say, "Hi, this is Lori, the woman with the van."

She says, "Hi, how are you doing? Oh, just a minute please."

I can hear her turn up the T.V. and then she yells, "Oh my fucking God!!! Oh my God!!!"

I said, "What? Are you okay?" I thought someone was robbing her. I didn't know what was going on and she was freaking.

She says, "I can't talk right now. The owner is on T.V."

So we run and turn on the T.V. and they are talking
about this woman who was driving with her husband, they were chased off of the freeway in the
desert by her lover, who I guess had been threatening her and making her life miserable.   So she and
her husband were trying to escape somewhere.
This jealous lover ran them off the freeway, put a
gun to the head of the husband and shot him point
blank. So this is a live eye cam of the police taking
her out of the desert, and they arrested her boyfriend, and her husband is dead. And this is the
lady whom we had just called to see if we could
buy the van from. I'm like oh my God, maybe we
can get it really cheap. I couldn't believe it. We
had to buy this van. And this lady did sell it to us.
It was so fucking weird. We ended up leaving after
about five days, we had finally settled with the van,
and went and bought it.

Angie: That doesn't even sound real.

Lori: I know.

Angie: But I don't think you could make that up.

Lori: No. I have witnesses. And so we bought the
van and that was that. That was our tour van.

Angie: Do you still have it?

Lori: Actually we just sold it in October.

Big Drill Car

"...the Dodge
dealer cleared
the showroom,
and we set up
under a picture
of Lee Iacocca."

BIG DRILL CAR

Interviewed by Greg Jacobs on the phone with
Frank Daly (vocals)

Frank: It was in Wisconsin, we were driving
from......I'm stoned.......uh, from Eau Claire, WI to
St. Louis, MO. And we had two days to get there so
naturally we left late. And we just figured we
would breeze right through and get to St. Louis in
about eleven hours. So we started to drive down the
highway. We'd been driving about two hours and
the van started to act up. It wasn't running right,
so we limped into a Dodge dealership in Madison,
WI. It was still about an eight hour drive from
Madison to St. Louis. So we had a couple hours, so
we could wait for the van to get fixed. So we were
sitting there at the dealership, and one of the guys
there listened in on a conversation and figured out
that we were a band and that we were kind of
pressed for time, stuff like that. So it was starting
to look like we couldn't figure out what was wrong
with the van and it wasn't gonna be ready in time
for us to make it to the show in St. Louis.

So,, a guy named Dwight Perry, who played, inci-
dentally, on the '72 Miami Dolphins, owned the
dealership. And he said: "Hey, I understand that
you guys are a band and I want to throw a party
here so, how much money would it cost for us to
get you guys to play here?" We agreed that we
would play for the price of the van being fixed,
which was a couple hundred bucks. So he went out,
and he rented a P.A.. He cleared the showroom and
we set up in the showroom in front of a picture of

Lee Iacocca. And played for about an hour and a half to about five salesmen and about six really bummed out car shoppers! And uh, that's the whole story. And that was the last show of our tour. We drove straight home from there.

Greg: Were people just freaking out when they walked in and saw you guys playing?

Frank: Well, yeah. There was like a couple old people that came in, and looked and like plugged their ears and walked out of the show room.

Greg: So you were 'Hallraking?'

Frank: Yeah! We totally 'Showroom raked!' (laughs)

Buck Pets

"And they were
all waiting for
Jane's Addiction
to come out the
back door. There
were hundreds of
people waiting
there to beat
them up."

BUCK PETS

Told by Ian Beech

One time we were in Chicago playing at the Metro
with Smashing Pumkins. Ray Washman (drummer
for Scratch Acid, etc) came to see us, we had just
met him that night and he was from Texas, too. So
after the show we were hanging out with him and
talking about Texas, and a friend of ours who was
on tour with us had walked up to the bar. Somehow he got into some trouble with a couple of guys
at the bar, they started hassling him for no reason
(so he said). So we hung around in the club for a
little while, and then everybody cleared out, but
there were still a couple people there, including
these two guys that were hassling him.

They split after a while, and we follwed them
upstairs, thinking nothing of it. When we get up to
the top of the stairs, and outside, we get jumped by
six skinheads. So we're thinking, "Oh, this is great,
there's four of us and six of them." So what happened then, jeez, it was just a flurry of fists and shit
and Ray Washman just started kicking some butt.
He was fighting three people at once! And beating
them! It was pretty amazing to watch; one guy
from Texas kicking ass. So somehow we managed
to get a couple of them on the ground, and we got
in our van and we were about to drive away. And
Ray Washman was standing there, still fighting
three guys at once, while we were pulling away.
"Okay Ray, you can jump in the van now!" And he's
like "No it's okay I'm just staying a few blocks
away," and he's still fighting these guys and we're

like, "Okay see you later, nice meeting you."

And as we're pulling away, one of the guys came running up to the van window and he was trying to grab our road manager, who was like 300 pounds. So our road manager just clocks the guy and he goes flying. We were all laughing.

But two weeks later, when we ran out of money in the middle of the desert and we hadn't eaten in two or three days, we caught our road manager in a bathroom stall eating B-grade puffed fucking cheetos out of a bag! He was keeping food from us. I mean he's a nice guy but I don't know what was going through his brain. We didn't have any money to eat and here he was in a bathroom stall eating potato puffs or cheese puffs or something. It was pretty hilarious.

One time we were in a giant riot when we toured with Jane's Addiction. This was the second time we toured with them; I don't know why they asked us the second time. The first time was pretty fun, but when they went out the second time the band was just a wreck, and Perry was a wreck. We got into this riot in Philadelphia, after Jane's Addiction played only fifteen minutes. We played first, but only got to play about fifteen minutes, because they were sreaming for us to get off the stage. Tickets for this show were $20, and in Philadelphia, no one has money, it's totally depressed. So for Jane's Addiction to charge $20 and only play 15 minutes, and the opening band to play 15 minutes.... There were a couple thousand kids running around in the streets, and they scraped up Jane's Addiction's tour bus and paddy wagons were called in. And they were all waiting for Jane's Addiction to come out the back door, there were hundreds of people waiting there to beat them up! We have it all on video.

Buffalo Tom

"Then she goes "hchtoo" and spits right in my face. So I spit right back at her."

BUFFALO TOM

Interviewed by Greg Jacobs and Gary Hustwit back stage at Sound FX in San Diego, CA.

Bill: In Europe, in France, this girl was attacking me while I was on stage. She was grabbing me, with my guitar still on and the guitar was just going "clang! clang!" She was spitting too. She spit on me. She was a stud. She had, uh, she was bald, a skinhead. Well I was getting hit with beer all throughout the set. And I said: "Please stop throwing beer at us. You know we don't really like that." I knew it was like a rock and roll thing and I let it go for a long time. But we were starting to get completely drenched. And we were about to start another song and she came up going: "Nananananananananana"

She was drunk as hell. I didn't know if it was her that was throwing it. But, she said: "I thought it would refresh you! I thought that it would be refreshing for you!" I said "No, No, No!" Then she goes "hchtoo" and spit right in my face. So I spit right back at her. So she starts coming after me, scratching at me, grabs the guitar and it was clanging.

Gary: Is this during a song?

Bill: No this was right before a song. All the people are going " Hey, hey, hey!" And we left the stage after that. We came back out eventually because it was really early when we walked off. It was just insane. And we came back, cause people pay a lot of money, people paid like, the equivalent of $20.00 just to see a rock show, in some shitty little venue.

And when we came back on, we had to go outside
and come back into the club another way. And I
saw this guy, you know, really going at it, arguing
with these guys, these big bouncer guys. These big
bouncer guys were with dogs, like German Shep-
herds, they were serious, man. And these were just
rock guys. And then we heard the other night,
some guy came back stage and said: "You know
they gave her electric shock." And we go: "With a
stun gun?" and he goes: "Yes, electric shock!"

Butthole Surfers

"We then
verbally and
mentally
assaulted each
person in the
audience until
they left the
room."

BUTTHOLE SURFERS

As told by King Coffey (drummer).

Well, here's my half anecdote before going into the
full anecdote. The oddest period of our touring
periods was when we were touring with Cathlene,
who was our performance artist. She would per-
form virtually naked while we played, with white
paint over her body and silver tin foil on her teeth.
She was also a highly spiritual woman who was
really into religion. But the thing is she was in-
venting her own religion as she marched along.
Part of it included one year of not speaking.
Whenever she had to communicate she would write
stuff down on a piece of paper. One time I asked
her, "Cathlene, can you tell me why you are not
speaking anymore?" And she paused, and she
paused, and she paused, and finally she wrote
down on a piece of paper, "Well...its hard to say."
That's my half anecdote.

My full anecdote of the weirdest bill I recall was in
Stuvongurt, Norway (consult atlas, West Coast). It
was when we had Kramer in the band. We were
scheduled to play in Stuvongurt, Norway. We were
billed as being Shockabilly, because of Kramer.
And for some inexplicable reason Shockabilly are
really popular in Norway.

So when we showed up and it was just the Butthole
Surfers, everybody was disappointed. They were
saying (delivered in a bad Norwegian/German
accent), "Where's Shockabilly!? Kramer...is this
your new band?"

He said, "No. No. This is a band from Texas. I'm

just playing for them now...blah, blah, blah...They're really good though! You'll like them!"

By the time we hit the stage its in front of like twenty people, because by then, everyone wanted their money back because it wasn't Shockabilly. So there are twenty people in this room and they all look like they play for that band Aha, right? They stood in the back corner of the room with arms folded. We began to play a song, but then we realized that the whole thing was completely ludicrous. So then we began making noise, just straight ahead noise, we refused to play music. We then verbally and mentally assaulted each member of the audience until they left the room. Finally, when we got everybody to leave the room, we played the songs to amuse ourselves. If somebody tried to creep back in, we would then start making noise again and assault the people some more, both with words and eventually bottles and stuff. We intentionally drove everyone out of the room, and played a set for no people.

There was also the time we played for people in Seattle, and we actually outnumbered the people in the audience. We again had realized how ludicrous the situation was, so we encouraged all four people to come up to the stage and we introduced the audience to themselves. "What is your name? Joe? Okay. What is your name? Mary? Okay, Joe meet Mary!" That was the first tour, back in 1983.

Cadillac Tramps

"They were walking towards me, man, saying, "You got the mojo, You got the mojo." And, uh, I started screaming for the nurse..."

CADILLAC TRAMPS

Gabby (vocals) interviewed by Greg Jacobs.

Gabby: Ok, we were in New Orleans, we played and we met some friends out there. The next night we played in Baton Rouge but I went back to New Orleans (after the show) with some friends of mine. We stopped off at this all black cemetery, and went running around the tombstones. We were having a good time. It was a really cool cemetery. You know how, in New Orleans, everything floats, kind of? Everything's in these crypts; we were crawling around on these crypts, and screwing around and at that time I got stung by these mosquitoes. They were like dirty swamp mosquitoes.

The next day I came down with this thing called Farentitus. You get it from the mosquitoes. I started getting a little headache and about an hour after, I was completely out. I blacked out. I woke up in the hospital. I had like 106.2 degree temperature, or something like that. So the nurse was saying, "You better be real careful, you gotta take your clothes off. We might have to put you in intensive care." Then, all of a sudden I started seeing dead black people in my hospital room. It literally looked like these dead people were coming after me. They were walking towards me, man, saying "You got the mojo, you got the mojo. You were fucking with us." And, uh, I started screaming for the nurse and she came in my room. I kinda grabbed her shirt, and kinda pulled her toward me and, I was wigging out, and accidentally unbuttoned a couple of her buttons, you know. (Laughs) It's called "The Dirty Swamp Disease."

Greg: So did you have to go home? Or did you recover and finish the tour?

Gabby: No, no, we had two days after that in Austin, TX and Houston, TX. You know man, every time we're out, we've got a great thing going in Houston and Austin, we've got a real strong following out there. The last time we were out (on tour) our van broke down before we hit Austin. So we had to sell it to some guy for $60.00 and we missed those two shows (Austin and Houston). Then this time out, that Dirty Swamp Thing happened. So I went home for a couple days (to recover), then we finished the tour and went up into Canada.

Greg: When was that? What tour?

Gabby: That was the last one. The Tombstone Radio Tour (Nov 92).

Chune

"The next thing
I see is a car
coming straight
at us, and
bingo! Chune is
in the spin
cycle..."

CHUNE

The fifteen minute Chune tour in '94

Just like the great Willy Nelson says, "On the road
again, I just can't wait to get on the road again;" or
something like that. In our case we wanted to live
Willy's words...honkeytonks, hotel rooms, fancy
cocktails and whores. Sounds like we know what
we're talking about, right? Well, we don't. This
was to be our first tour; virgins on a new scene,
excited virgins at that. All the way from our home
in San Diego, CA to Vancouver Canada. May not
sound like a lot to you tour veterans, but to some
simple guys from El Cajon (a suburb of S.D. with
deep white trash roots), you may as well have sent
us to Pakistan. Many preparations had been made
for this two and a half week round up. The day to
leave had finally arrived and we were ready to go.
Our first show was in San Luis Obispo and we were
leaving at high noon and the thought of Los Angeles traffic had us more nervous than a long tailed
cat in a room full of rocking chairs. We decided on
the Interstate 15 North to avoid some of that L.A.
shit. We were about 15 minutes into our long
awaited tour with Lance M. at the wheel, Tony S.
sitting shot gun, and Andy H. (me) behind Lance.
Our friend Andrew M. was behind Tony and Mike
T. was in the loft we had built for sleeping. All of a
sudden there seemed to be a stampede all around
us, and then I heard Lance say, like a pilot to his
crew, "hold on boys we're going down!!" The next
thing I see is a car coming straight towards us, and
bingo! Chune is in the spin cycle, up and down and
all around we went. When it was all over we had

rolled the van 6 times and slid upside down for
more than 50 yards. That was it. Our first tour
was over in about 15 minutes. I guess we were
lucky because everybody was okay for the most
part and only half the equipment was thrown onto
the freeway. You win some, you lose some, and I
guess the honkeytonks and whores will have to
wait until another day.

Circle Jerks

"And the club owner's like, "Here I got something for you," and reaches into his desk and pulls out a gun..."

CIRCLE JERKS

Greg Hetson interviewed by Greg Jacobs.

Are we rolling? O.K. I believe it was about 1983, on
a Circle Jerks tour, playing at the Electric Banana
in Pittsburgh, Pennsylvania. That place has been a
punk rock club forever, obviously. I think it's still
there. We were playing a gig and, I don't know, we
had maybe a $500 guarantee at the time. So we're
playing the gig, we're having a good time, we're
all getting drunk and the club owner's having a
great time. He's got a pretty packed crowd on like a
Thursday or Wednesday. And our bass player at the
time was Earl Liberty, he used to be in Saccharin
Trust; he's played the club a few times and the
owner's like, "Oh, I love Earl". They were getting
along and having a good 'ol time. So Earl goes in
the back room at the end of the night to settle up;
he was doing our tour managing as well as playing
bass. The more and more they were drinking after
the show, the more bitter and angry the owner was
getting and he's like, "I don't know if we should
pay you the rest of your money." We had like $250
advance which had been sent up to the booking
agency or whatever, so he goes, "I'm not going to
pay you, you don't deserve it." And Earl goes, "Yeah
right, you're joking." He goes, "I ain't joking," and
they go back and forth and Earl still thinks the guy
is joking because 20 minutes earlier he was Earl's
best buddy saying, "Yeah, we should have you here
every week, you pull in a good crowd." And then
obviously, Earl's beginning to think that the guy
might be serious because the he's like, "Yeah, get
the fuck out of my office," and shit like that. Then

Earl goes, "No, we're going to get paid." And the owner's like, "Here I got something to show you." He reaches into the desk and pulls out a gun and starts waving it so Earl's going, "Hey man, mellow out." Then the booking agent comes in, it's this woman who's booking the club, and she says, "what's going on here?" And the owner says, "I ain't paying these guys, tell them to fuck off," and he's still waving the gun and Earl's like, "O.K. I'm getting the hell out of here, later." And the booking agent says as they're walking out, "Don't worry about it, I'll make sure you get the money." And the owner runs after her waving the gun yelling, "You ain't paying them nothing. If you pay them any more money I'm going to shoot you." So basically we all jumped into the van and Earl's yelling, "The guy's got a gun, let's get the fuck out of here."

But we did get the extra $250. And we never played the Electric Banana again. When other bands go through and they ask him, "Is it true that you pulled a gun on the Circle Jerks?" He always says "Those goddamn Circle Jerks, going around the country saying I pulled a gun on them. Bring them back here. I'll show them what a real man will do!"

That's basically the story.

Coffin Break

"I just kind
of went,
"Oh well, fuck,"
and just kept
stirring my
coffee..."

COFFIN BREAK

Dave (drummer) was interviewed by Greg Jacobs.

Dave: Well, let's see....Coffin Break.....We've done quite a bit of touring, We've done five major U.S. tours, and lots of West Coast deals. But our first tour, we came down to San Francisco for a couple of shows. We drive a '69 Dodge van. And we were driving all night long, back (to Seattle). And we pulled over and fell asleep in this rest area, right? I got up (some hours later) and drove to a gas station. And these guys were still asleep, up on the loft, in the back (of the van). They were all laying in the back. It was just the three of us. I went in to get some coffee, I'm in there, in this AMT pouring coffee. Just sitting there, putting a little cream in there and this guy comes in and says: "Uh, are you driving a white van?" And I said "Yeah" and I looked out the window where I parked. You could see (the van from inside). And it was gone! The guy said "It's rolling down the street!" It just kind of rolled back, out onto the street. I just kind of sat there going "Well, fuck, what am I supposed to do? Run out of this door and chase it down the block? I don't know. Dive in front of it or something?" I just kind of went: "Oh, well, fuck." I just kept stirring my coffee and it drove back up . Those guys woke up. Well, Pete woke up and he dove over all the shit and the seats and then hit the breaks with his hands, you know? Cause he had just bolted out of bed. So he just got up and drove it back in and that was how they woke up (laughs). They woke up rolling out of the parking lot, down the street, they came pretty close to going into this big ditch but they didn't.

The Cult

"And we are
tearing across
it in a golf
cart, in the
rain, and Ian
overturns it
into a lake. We
run back,
however, and
steal another
one."

THE CULT

Well, this one's about, I suppose this is one of my favorites, one of the funniest laughs I ever had. It doesn't always sound so funny saying it as it was there, which is kinda' one of those things I suppose. Its about trying to steal an airplane with The Cult. This is when we were supporting Billy Idol on the Electric Tour, and we'd been given two days off in a place called Lake Geneva in Wisconsin, which is a golfing resort. All together there must have been fifteen (people) in the crew and band, including Idol and the Cult's lot.

We were staying at a golfing hotel with absolutely nothing to do but drink, 'cause I think about four people out of the fifteen played golf. There's a little lake at the resort and the first day off was alright. We rented some of those jet ski things and we played on them. I crashed one and sunk it: the first person to sink a jet ski. We were then banned from using them.

So the second day there was nothing to do what so ever. Everyone started drinking about...I Don't know...pretty early, breakfast. There were a few fans and stuff knocking around. There was a guy on the tour with us called John Miller. And John Miller was a mercenary, he was the Cult's security guy. He actually wrote a book himself, he was like an x-SAS soldier who'd been on the road as well, and he was like the biggest scammer you'd ever met. You could never believe anything he said. He was always trying to put one over on anyone. So we have this guy on the road with us, this guy who had kidnapped "*Ronnie Beaks*" from Brazil and took

him to Jamaica and tried to get a ransom for him
from the English government. I don't know if
you've ever heard of a guy called *Lord Lucan*, but
John Miller was also the one who had set up this
whole scam about the fact that he had found *Lord
Lucan*. Lord Lucan was the guy whose Nanny was
found dead, and he disappears and has never been
seen again. So all these crappy newspapers in
England, you know the *Enquirer* type were con-
tacted by John Miller and he told them all that he
had found Lord Lucan. He got a load of money out
of them and told them to come to Jamaica, he set
up this entire scam. Anyway, this is our security
guy, just to give you a rough idea of what he was
like.

We're in this golfing hotel, its about eight or nine
o'clock at night and its raining, it has been raining all day and everyone is really bored and really
drunk. There are absolutely no women within
about fifty miles of this fucking hotel, because we
are in the middle of nowhere. Ian at this time, he's
sober now of course, but he was drinking a lot then
to say the least, we all were.

In this particular instance there was myself, Ian,
John Miller, and this guy called Jon (yawn) who
was the money guy, this little Jewish guy who was
really funny. Ian decided that he wanted to steal a
golf cart and learn how to drive cause he couldn't
drive and he still can't drive. So we go out to this
parking lot around the back and all of the Golf
carts have been chained up. Miller goes off and
finds a hack saw blade and comes back and starts
sawing through this steel chain. This security guy
from the hotel comes up to us and asks us what
we're doing and all this. We say we're out here
standing in the rain 'cause Ian the singer is getting

hassled by all these fans and the security guard is going to have to go in and move them. The security guy completely falls for it and goes back inside, which gives us enough time to steal a golf cart. So we all jump in this golf cart, its pouring rain and we're all really drunk.

Now, this is like a Jack Nicholas designed golf course, they spent thirty thousand dollars on each putting green to get it right. D'ya know what I mean? And we are tearing across it in a golf cart, in the rain, like ripping it up, and driving about, and Ian overturns the thing into a lake. We run back however and steal another one. So we're driving around again and we see this big fence. Miller then says that he has always wanted to do that thing they do in the Westerns, where they drive through the fences. So we decide to drive in and out of this fence, making fucking great big holes in it, but eventually that gets boring as well.

By this time, however, someone's obviously caught on to what's happening, and there's all these police cars driving across the golf course trying to find us and there's all these lights going, but we are just laughing and giggling, thinking its all really funny. We abandon the golf cart and this is where John Miller takes over in his little military style operations.

We are all crawling on our bellies through this long grass trying to get away from the police. We crawl all the way back to the hotel and we are laughing our fucking faces off and Ian decides that he hasn't had enough fun yet, he wants to steal another one. So we go out and steal another golf cart, and we drive down this little country lane which eventually leads to this airport. It is somewhat like a crop spraying airport, with a few little,

I don't know, Cessna type planes. John Miller then informs us that he can hotwire an airplane if we would like to go for a plane ride. Everyone is like, of course we do! So we open one of these planes up, he jumps in the cockpit, and he is seriously trying to jumpstart this plane. Then the police come barreling down the highway. And Ian is just sitting there gurgling, he's so fucking drunk, while the police surround us in this plane. Miller, being as calm as can be, says, "whatever you do, deny everything." We are sitting there in the plane, caught red fucking handed, and Miller tells the police that we are just trying to get away from the fans. At this point we are about four miles from the hotel. The police subsequently take us back to the hotel, they don't do anything about the airplane, we talk our way out of everything saying that we are just trying to get away from the hotel. When we arrive with the police back at the hotel, the hotel manager is going absolutely fucking mad because we destroyed his golf course.

We are immediately thrown out of the hotel and by this time it is about two o'clock in the morning. So we are just standing there with nowhere to go, it is pouring rain, and there are no hotels for miles. We end up sleeping on the tour bus. The next morning Miller is telling us that no matter what happens deny all. The tour manager then comes banging on the door. He is a rather stuck-up English guy called Barry Mead. He is asking us who is responsible for what happened, going down a list of damages including thirty thousand dollars to the greens, seven-hundred dollars to the fence, three golf carts. And he is asking who is going to pay for everything. We kept denying everything, saying we were framed, it wasn't us. The tour manager

eventually knocked the bill down to four or five
thousand dollars and that was about it really for
the airplane story. I don't know if you can make it
sound any funnier in words, but it was very funny
at the time, I don't think I laughed so hard in all
my life.

Descendents

"So the next day, it had snowed that night, and Milo decided he was gonna drive..."

DESCENDENTS

Bug Phace (roadie) interviewed by Greg Jacobs in ALL's tour bus.

Bug: Descendents tour, Gooch road managing, we were in Wisconsin. We just played Appleton. We stayed at the promoters house. So the first thing he (the promoter) told me was: "No one's allowed in the basement. My parents have a stash of liquor down there."

So, where do you think I went right away! I'm sleeping down there in the basement! So the next day, it had snowed that night, and Milo decided he was gonna drive. There was a driveway straight behind us (across the street) so all he had to do was back straight up with the trailer, and back into the other drive way, like normal. But he decided that he was gonna make the cut on the street with the trailer, instead of backing straight up. There was only like two inches, three inches of snow on the ground. You know those colber pipes that go underneath people's driveways and they have a ditch at the end of their yard? Well, he cuts the trailer, backs it through the guy's yard, his parent's house, into the ditch, and dug two big old fuckin'ruts from the trailer tires. They went down through the yard, into the ditch. And he just looked at me really crazy, with big eyes, put it in park, got out, ran into the house and started peeking through the fucking curtains. While me, Gooch and Bill were trying to get it out. Man, he *really* fucked up the kid's yard.

Doughboys

"Dear Penthouse
Letters, I
couldn't believe
any of your
letters,
until..."

DOUGHBOYS

Interview by Greg Jacobs on the phone with
Jonathan "Widdalee" Cummins.

Widallee: We were driving down the road and as
you know, we have a Ford Econo-Line with a U-
Haul trailer on the back. This is a completely, 100%
true story! Newman (drummer) was at the wheel,
and we were all just finally falling asleep. We were
going to our first show, actually, just leaving Quebec. No, we left Guelph and we were going home to
Quebec. We had just finished playing a show with
Change of Heart. Suddenly, as I'm just falling
asleep, the van starts moving around. I woke up,
as you usually do. And it was just, like when big
trucks pass you, the air just kind of pushes the van
to the side and we started going "Wholly-Fuck!"
And Newman couldn't come out of the spin after
the big truck went beside us and stuff. He was
trying to correct it but, because of the weight on
the trailer, we just started...and it was totally snow-
ing, like mega.....and so the roof of the U-Haul just
ripped off, and all of our amps, huge amps, started
sprawling all over...ripped right through...like a
whole wall of the U-Haul got ripped right out. The
whole roof flew off and all of our equipment was
like completely strewn all over this major highway.
It was 3 o'clock in the morning. We got out and
went "AHHHHHH!" And Change of Heart were
about ten minutes behind us and they were driving
along and they said " Hey, didn't that thing over
there look like a Marshall Stack?" And they were
going "Yeah, yeah isn't that The Doughboys equipment?" And then they went "Holy Fuck!" And ev-

erybody was O.K. but, we had to basically pull all
of the equipment off of the highway and take it off
to the side before people started running over it.
And the best part of the story is......This has got to
start out...Dear Penthouse Letters, I couldn't believe
any of your letters until....That's how you're going
to have to start this story off. So there was this big
tractor trailer type of thing, and it pulls on to the
side of the highway and these two guys in white
leather fringe jackets and Farrah Fawcett (hair)do's
get out. They go "Hey we heard you guys had all
your equipment all over the highway, we heard it
on the C.B. (radio). Some trucker alerted us." And
we were going, "yeah, fuck, man, we have no way
of transporting it. Our van won't hold all of this
equipment." And they're going, "No problem." 'Cos
they had this huge tractor trailer. And then out
comes this girl with Harley Davidson, white jog-
ging shorts on, wearing, like those really bad,
Kemp worker glasses and stuff. She steps out and
goes, "Yeah, no problem, you guys can just put all
your stuff in the back of our thing." We were like:
"Cool!" And Change of Heart were helping us move
the equipment. And we opened up the back door to
the tractor trailer and there was this big poster
that said, "MISS NUDE UNIVERSE". And we looked
at the girl in the Harley Davidson shorts and it was
Miss Nude Universe! I even got the poster, I'll send
it along to you. So we opened up the trailer and
there were all these monkeys and stuff. There was a
monkey, a snake and a bunch of other weird, exotic
animals. And one of the guys was like, an animal
trainer, or something. And they worked it into her
show . They ended up driving us to a hotel, and we
stashed all of our equipment into a hotel room, and
she gave us all posters. She said that the next time
we play Las Vegas she'll come down and see us.

Greg: Explain again how the accident started.

Widallee: There was a big huge tractor trailer truck, you know, like there's tons of them on the highway, and it just booted down the highway. Every time one passes us going really fast, the air current kind of pushes our van opposite the truck. . It did that and then Newman tried to correct it by putting it back on the road. 'Cos the van started going off the road, as it does slightly (when a big truck passes). But it made the U-Haul trailer totally start sliding way to the right and he was trying to correct the trailer and get it back on the road, but the more he was trying to correct it, the more we were all over the road.

Greg: So you actually slid?

Widallee: (To Pat) We made it to the side of the road right? (To Greg) O.K. We pulled over to the side of the road after he had controlled it, looked in the rear view mirror and saw all of our amps and drums on the highway. We just started going "Fuck! Everybody get up!" And everybody was like, in shock. One of the guys, this roadie who has with us, said that that was his last show with us,

He didn't want to do anymore shows with us after that. He was totally freaked-out! The guy was just totally freaked-out! Fuck it was weird! And it was freezing too, it was soooo cold. It was insane. And then we just got a (new) U-Haul trailer in the morning and went home.

The Dwarves

"...suddenly the lights went up, the music went off and they were like, "The Dwarves have to leave!" over the loudspeaker."

THE DWARVES

Blag Jesus was interviewed by Greg Jacobs over the phone, May 26, 1993.

Blag: We were in Switzerland with the Supersuckers and Reverend Horton Heat and there was a big bunch of us all going around when we played this show. People got kind of pissed off, they didn't really do anything, but then after the show this one person took us to a disco. When we got there, we noticed that all the people who were in the disco were the people that had been running the club. So everyone looked around real weird when we came in. We were out on the dance floor like dancing around and suddenly the lights went up, all the music went off and over the loudspeaker we heard, "The Dwarves have to leave!" And we were like, fuck! We just thought it was kind of funny, and we were giving them shit. Then the Supersuckers started scuffling with some of the guys. Everything got really hectic and everyone started running around. Somebody from one of the groups put a big milk crate through a plate-glass window of the place. It sounded like a huge gunshot. There was a bang, everybody stopped, and we took off running. We ran back to the bus and told them to drive on to France. We had to get the fuck out of Switzerland 'cause there was going to be some shit.

New Jersey. I took acid in New Jersey and we played this show and Vadge Moore went really crazy. Everyone was fighting around and there weren't that many people and we weren't that happy about it. All these "East Coasty" type people were standing there being weird and I was all hippy-trippy and I didn't care, all this shit was going down. But Vadge Moore like bashed out all these lights. A security guy got up and grabbed Vadge''s drums and threw them at him. We got all this on film. He threw his floor tom, his tom-tom at him from the back and it smashed into him. Then Crash Landon came out and started attacking him. That was the weirdest one, getting attacked by his own drum set. I didn't even realize it was going on. I was looking at the deli tray for inner meaning.

The dirtiest stories are the fuck stories, but I can't...just in case there are any illegitimate children, its tough to really elaborate on them. But see...I can't puss out as much as the other bands.

One time we were in Lawrence, playing with Unrest, and a certain band, with a notoriously skanky chick in it who lives in New York. I had never met her before and everyone on the tour just hated these guys. I guess Unrest and this band were driving around in a station wagon for five weeks, just stinking drunk. They were pretty nasty by then it was Halloween and everyone was frying. I saw her fighting with her boyfriend; I started laughing and walked over there. I was wearing this see-through leotard to play in and I asked her to help me put it on. She was like, "Okay." So we went in our van and just immediately, like thirty seconds after I met her, I'm fucking her in the van. I came immediately, it was really nauseating, after like thirty seconds. Her boyfriend is banging on the door of the van. I just throw her off of me, she doesn't realize I'm through yet. I opened up the van door, he grabs her, throws her on the ground

and starts punching her. And he is yelling, "You
bitch! You bitch!" They were in the van together, I
just pushed them out of the car and left, went on
my way and did the show.

Later on we were eavesdropping on their conversation. She was saying, "Well...I just wanted something real!" That's probably the best story I can
think of off hand.

Ethyl Meatplow

"That night I didn't get any stitches, but I did get a concussion, and soft tissue damage to the throat..."

ETHYL MEATPLOW

John Napier interviewed by Gary.

On the Nitzer Ebb tour, which was the very first tour that we barely pulled through, we were on our way to Seattle and the catalytic converter in our van went out. We just happened to be in front of a military outpost, and pulled up right in front of the main gate. There were two army fellows standing at attention, saluting everyone as they arrived for work. We jump out of the van and we are ragged, fucked looking! We say, "Hey! Can You help us?"(One of those special, awkward moments-ed.). Anyway, that is not the point, back to the van.

The four of us traveling together would not all fit in the tow truck. One of us would have to stay on board the van and hide while being towed. Of course I was volunteered. I said "fuck it," and hid in the van. He put it up on the tow bar and we were on the way, everything was cool. We were headed for a garage where someone can fix the van, and the van.........falls off the tow bar....with me in it. And I'm not supposed to be in there, and I start thinking that I am going to die! And every-one in the tow truck besides the driver, is thinking I'm going to die. Everyone kept their mouth shut, though, and I'm alive, but it was fucking nuts! Then I had to stay in the van and just rough it, and I had pissed my pants!

On the three tours that we've done this year, I've gotten...uh...thirteen stitches, in different places on my head! Starting with Wichita, people were lifting me up, and then they got tired of lifting me.

So they just dropped me...on the back of my head. Then, in Minneapolis, as soon as the back of my head was healed I got punched in the front of my head by this guy in Pachenko (spelling) from Wisconsin, who were playing a show with us.

On the first tour I also jumped off of a very tall stage, about an eight foot stage. I landed on my heels, and drove them into my feet (ouch-ed.).

Well, there is also always the problem with security guards. I'm always either being force fed bullshit by security, or just beat up by security guards. My dick speaks for me, always wanting to dry hump them. Sometimes I make them hold my microphone, which they're not too happy about, but they get into it after awhile.

I was down watching Zeni Geva play one night at the Whiskey, before we were to play. And I wasn't doing anything, man, I was just standing there. I wasn't being a spastic, ya' know, like I usually am. But everyone was freaking out, it was totally packed, and this security guard comes up the stairs and jabs me really fucking hard in my belly with his flashlight (from John's tone, one may still detect a little anger-ed.). The guard starts blurbing something, but I can't hear shit 'cause its like Zeni Geva playing, right? So I pointed to my hand stamp that band members who are playing that night get, and he pushes me really hard. I raise my hand open fisted and point to my stamp once again. The next thing I know a flashlight hits me across my forehead, I'm down on the ground, he is on top of me, has me in a headlock and is trying to drag me to the back fire escape exit! I gather he wanted to throw me down and get rid of me. That's what I get for wanting to see Zeni Geva.

The guard ended up quitting his job because of stress. Later that night, one of the girls in Crash Worship was assaulted both verbally and physically by the same guard. Bambi of the Mudwimmin' got shit from security, along with Carla (of Ethyl Meatplow) as well. So it definitely wasn't just me, being me.

That night I didn't get any stitches, but I did get a concussion, and soft tissue damage to the throat. It was the first show on the tour, before we even left town. We had wanted it to be special...

3 Little Nightmares

#1 It was the first week of the tour and we were opening up for a fashion show in Detroit with Foreskin 500. All of the people there were in suits. They seemed upset about having to talk over the noise of the music. I jumped up on top of one of their tables during the set and they just kept right on talking.

#2 We were setting up to play in Rhode Island, and we are told by the manager that we have to get off stage early for Reggae Frat Night!!! "You don't want to be on stage when 'The Bus' arrives," he says. Foreskin 500 took off their clothes and they stopped the show before we played anyway.

#3 Boston...Access Club...Metal Night. Sure enough it was metal night, the poodle hairdos were in excess. The first question from the doorman to Steak was, "There's not gonna be any queers here tonight, are there?"

Mike Watt

"After a couple hours of sleep I awoke to find one of my balls had blown up to the size of a softball!"

fIREHOSE/ MINUTEMEN

....Tour stories faxed in from Mike Watt.

Mike Watt's
WEIRD TOUR HELLS

Touring has presented many interesting situations
to me. Here's some real-life happenings in the life
of one driven punk rocker.

GUN FUN - In the summer of 1984 the MINUTEMEN
did a gig in Columbia, SC during the CAMPAIGN
TRAIL tour. After the gig, we went to this dude's
house. He had naked pictures of his wife on the
walls and shit like that. After some beers, we're
laying on the living room floor ready to crash
when he tells us, "Well, you guys can start fucking
whenever you want." I said, "What?!" Then he
says, "I got a shotgun in that other room." George
says, " I bet I'll get to it before you do." This
asshole then flies. George goes and sleeps out on
the porch. Me and D. Boon konk right there without moving. George says we just tried "sleep it off."

HEAD FLAME - The day before fIREHOSE's HAHD
KOA tour in the spring of 1987, my parked VW van
caught fire with my head in the engine compart-
ment. Luckily, when my head caught fire, I yanked
the Laker t-shirt I was wearing over my head and

this extinguished the fire. Unluckily, I had to start a six week tour the next day and had to play with my ear/nose/lip all burned up and full of pus. After each gig, Dav-o (our soundman then) would purge the bugs in my sores with hydrogen peroxide. The burning and boiling from this chemical reaction was intense but I survived both the burns and the tour with few scars. Kids at the gigs would think I was dressing-up like Rambo for the show with my bandages, wounds and all!

TURD HOUSE - While on the first MINUTEMEN European tour at the beginning of 1983 (opening for BLACK FLAG), we stayed at a squatter's pad in Geneva, Switzerland. After drinking their home-made shine, they told us it was made from rotten fruit and shit that they found in the dumpsters and garbage cans. I went to the head but since this was a squat, there hadn't been any water so there was no plumbing. The turds in that closet must have been piled up three feet high off the toilet! The stench overpowered me, twisting my face and throwing me to the floor. I pissed my pants but somehow managed to shut the door. I cannot relate accurately the reek of that stink.

BASS SNAP - During the LITTLE BIG tour in the spring of 1988, fIREHOSE played Charleston, SC where I bought the Salman Rushdi book, "The Satanic Verses." That night I used a strange bass for the gig, a Hagstrom which is made in Sweden. In the middle of the set, the headstock of the bass just snapped off while I was playing, sticking splinters of wood into me with the force of the fracture! After the gig, the Rushdi book was missing - disappeared. I never tried to get the book again; one does not fuck with Allah!

STOOGE ROUST - In the middle of the MINUTEMEN's CO-CONSPIRATORS tour in the fall of 1985, I went to pick Kira up at Newark Airport after soundcheck (we were playing in Manhattan, NYC). That whole tour I was wearing army clothes with a beard - sort of a Castro parody. Anyway, at the airport there was construction on a new addition and these automatic doors would not open. When I opened them myself, two plain clothes police grabbed me and threw me against a counter and completely (COMPLETELY!) searched me saying, "All right, what's up with you, Mr. Iranian!"

BALL SWELL - In the middle of the BUMRUSH THE SIDEMOUSE tour (Winter, 1988) fIREHOSE was playing Milwaukee, WI with DOS (me and Kira's two bass only band). The DOS set was bad enough but after two fIREHOSE sets (yep, we had to play TWICE that night), I was nearly dead with fever and chills. The next night in Chicago after a couple hours of sleep I awoke to find one of my balls had blown-up to the size of a softball. It blew my mind! We dropped Kira off at the airport and drove to Champaign, IL. Immediately, after we hit town we took me to the hospital and the doctor said somehow I had contracted something from a bladder infection Kira had recently had. For the rest of the tour (three more weeks), I had to keep a hot water bottle constantly on the ball. I was chaffed like a motherfuck when we finished.

KNEE POP - I was born with bad knees. I've had a surgery on each one in my early twenties. In the fall of 1991, fIREHOSE was on the LIVE TOTEM POLE tour and playing Chicago, IL with RUN WESTY RUN. It was the last show we were doing with them after touring together a few weeks. Near the end during the encore their drummer Dan opened a beer and sprayed it all over me. I slipped in the beer and dislocated my knee while rolling my ankle and spraining it; simultaneously I hit the deck and immediately went into shock, letting the bass go as I fell. The bass followed me down and hit me right in the mouth knocking one of my front teeth back about an inch and a half. Three blows with one hit! I put my knee back in its socket and reached in my mouth and yanked that tooth back to its original place. I had to do the touring sitting down with my knee the size of a casaba melon and my mind totally filled with pain and wretching. Then I had a six week Europe tour right after that! At least my tooth never fell out.

CHOW HEAVE - When I first started touring, food poisoning was a constant hazard. Now, with more than 20 tours under my belt, I got a gut like a turkey vulture (them road kill birds that fly over freeways). When the MINUTEMEN toured with REM in the winter of 1985, I got poisoned in Land-O-Lakes, FL. It became useless to keep changing my pants so I tied a shirt around my waist and rags around the bottoms of my pant legs, and just said fuck it. After three days my pants were full to the knees. Luckily, my condition soon improved. The first time fIREHOSE played the town where Edward went to college (Columbus, OH), I was poisoned right before the gig and had to play in a wailing fever and nausea. When we got done, he took me to his college buddy's pad and put me in his bed. My sickness took a turn for the worse and I suf-

fered in agony the whole night. Morning found
the bed I was in completely diarread and soiled.
What a way to meet Edward's buddies! I hope I
made an impression because the shame was total.

MOUTH FLAME- The SPRINGBOARD tour found
fIREHOSE playing Miami, FL in the spring of
1989. We were doing this gig in the Haitian area
where George had found some tiny orange peppers
and some brine shrimp. Not thinking much, I
chomped too many down and started burning
immediately. I tried flushing my mouth with
everything but nothing worked. I burned and
burned for minutes then hours! I played the gig
crying from them fucking peppers. They even
burned a hole in the roof of my mouth! To this day
my brain continues to leak from my mouth when I
open it.

Germs

"Darby said, 'No, I will never play here. When I dive off the stage these people aren't going to catch me.'"

GERMS

The Germs first and only tour (sort of) as told by
Nicole Panter (manager).

Darby, Lorna, Pat and I went up to San Francisco to
kind of do reconnaissance, and it happened to be
that while we were up there that weekend, Sid
killed Nancy. It was funny, in fact I think I still
have the t-shirt, there were people in front of
Mabuhay Gardens selling "Sid Murdered" com-
memorative t-shirts. We stayed in the San
Juan Hotel, which is this horrifying place, just up
from Mabuhay Gardens, that lots of bands stayed
at. It's really echoey inside and it's really third
world, and I think lots of Chinese People live there.
So like at 5:30 in the morning they all start waking
up and killing ducks or whatever it is they do. It
was really strange and weird, and I remember
Darby slept curled at the end of the bed, by my
feet! With all the people screaming in Chinese
inside this really echoey hotel, it gave the whole
weekend the quality of an opium dream.

At one point we went to a party at the Mutant's
Loft, which was in the loft district of San Francisco
at the time, I think it was the Mission District. We
were in the party and the police came knocking at
the door. Somebody said that if we just turn out
the lights and be very quiet, they'll go away. So we
turned out the lights, and were very quiet, and
three hours later they were still knocking...It was
really bizarre, and everyone was trying to pretend
that we weren't there.

Then, at the end of the weekend, I asked Darby

what he wanted me to do, whether or not he wanted me to book them into San Francisco. He just looked at me and said, "No. I will never play here. When I dive off the stage these people aren't going to catch me." So that was why the Germs never went out of town. They only played in L.A., they may have played in Camarillo once. Camarillo is a mental institution.

God Machine

"I don't think 20 minutes had passed before I was awakened by the sound of an animal dying in the corner of the room."

GOD MACHINE

As told by Phil Beaumont (road manager).

So we're three weeks into a tour of a very wet England, we finally have a night off in Liverpool, and actually a decent hotel to stay in; three star quality at five star prices, but decent nonetheless. Tomorrow night's promoter has put us all on the guest list to see a swirly lights and fog machine band, that will no doubt be wearing baggy jeans, excessive amounts of gold hoop earrings and donning hairstyles ala Julius Caesar. Thanks, but no thanks.

My sentiments aren't the same as everyone on the tour though. Realizing the show is a university gig brings the prospect of young influentials and very cheap beer, so the two guys I share a room with decide to go for the sake of a good piss up. Perfect for me; the room to myself means I only have to smell my own farts, watch the shitty T.V. program of my own choice and spend as long as I want in the bath.

This I do, and after a bit of relieving quality time with myself, I fall merrily to sleep. But the joy of slumber in a snoreless environment could never last forever. Around the ugly hours of the morning the door is opened by the giggles of my two beer filled roommates. Now one is much younger than the other, who has toured with plenty of other bands, a hired gun with more stories than respect for the sleeping. So the older guy scoffs at the idea of keeping quiet for my sake, and decides it would be fun to keep me awake until he goes to sleep. So sure enough the two drunken idiots are snoring away long before I can get cozy in my dreamland.

I don't think twenty minutes passed before I was awakened by the sound of an animal dying in the corner of the room. A worrying sound at the best of times, but when you realize it's the sound of your buddy learning how to puke its both unnerving and amusing at the same time. I sit up to make sure he is lying on his side and not pulling a Bonzo, Janis, Bon Scott et all, and wait until he passes out again.

Ten minutes later it's the sound of rain in the corner of the room. Once again it is the younger of the two drunks, he must have decided (unconscious as he was) that if he couldn't be rid of liquid through his mouth, a steady stream from the bowels would do the trick.

"Aaah, the sweet smell of revenge..." I thought when I realized he was pissing into my other roommates luggage.

For some stupid reason I tried to wake him and stop him, but soon realized I probably wouldn't be able to laugh this hard again for quite a while. So after he was done I basically giggled my ass to sleep, and dreamt of the mornings explanations.

After planting the seed in their minds that the strange smell in the room might be the subtle blend of urine on cotton, I split for a nice greasy breakfast. Soon enough I saw a hungover fellow enter a laundromat across the street with a rather soggy bag.

Kill Sybil

"...the woman
police officer
that looked like
John Denver in a
Farrah Fawcett
wig led me into
what would
become the room
of hell."

KILL SYBIL

This is a true story by Tammy Watson about the Kill Sybil "Blame it on the Meices" tour. It is such a horror story that I actually left things out instead of exaggerating.

The worst day of my life, on tour or otherwise:

By Tammy Ann Watson

Waking up to the smell of 4 pairs of 7 day old tube socks was not the best sign. Opening my swollen eyes to the bloated face of some guy from one of the bands we played with the night before I felt the world crashing in. The last thing I wanted to hear was, "Its check out time," and that was the first thing he said. Of course he had to slam the door and make my head explode. The sleazy Canadian motel room was filled with snoring men, two on the bed next to me, two or three on the floor and one next to me. As the only girl in the room I knew I had to get out of there before they stood up and revealed some part of their body that I would never want to see. The log next to me rolled over and shoved me. Apparently I was the only one woken up by mister red face's wake-up call. Standing up the smelly "rocked last night body funk" permeated my nostrils and I ran for the bathroom, knowing I was about to lose every drink I ever had. Managing to only step on one head and three feet on my way to the john, I hurled myself clean. As I am known for my loud vomiting, I woke the rest of the passed-out beasts up and missed their pale, pasty nudity, as they dressed while I puked. When I came back into the room I was greeted with so

many faces of sickly hung over boys that I figured I
was in hell or on tour with one too many bands.
All I could do was head for the patio and lament
ever agreeing to be a part of the label showcase in
a foreign country. I couldn't remember exactly
how much I had drank the night before or what
chemicals had made it into my system, and I definitely didn't want to think about how much I had
ingested in those short previous 5 days of the
"Blame it on the Meices Tour." Stumbling out,
everyone managed to group with their own bands,
as it is next to impossible to organize 30 hung over
punk rockers into 6 or 7 band vans. We even found
a place to eat god's gift to the terminally hungover;
two very greasy eggs, hashbrowns, burnt toast, and
diner coffee with that ever so replenishing large
glass of water. After the grease settled in I realized
the Kill Sybil van was full, meaning my band van
was full without me. The Meices were already
staying at my house on this tour of the northwest
and we were headed back to Seattle (home for a
show that night then off to finish the tour down
south) so I got in the van with them. This is where
the bad dream ended and the nightmare began.
Crackerbash decided to smoke the pot they had so
they wouldn't get busted at the border with it.
Good planning, so we joined in too. Of course we
didn't realize in our still drunk from the night
before state that it would mean being stoned out of
our simple little minds at the border crossing.
Quickly polishing off the "grass" we stonily rolled
to the border. We had nothing to fear but those
ever so friendly (sarcasm!) Canadian border police.
Once again I found myself in a small space with
four smelly men, but this time it was a van at an
international border. Almost immediately the
border police told us to pull it on over for inspec-

tion. 5 stoned hearts froze right then. Before we
even got out of the van the border dogs were pointing the "you've got illegal substances and must die"
finger right at us by running straight for the
yellow mini school bus/tour van. I thought I
would just pet the police pooches when they came
at me and sniffed my pot smoke soaked clothes and
say "they must smell my dog." But I didn't get the
chance. They put us into a waiting room with
about 10 official looking fucks staring right at us. I
got up to go pee, and the Mr. T wanna-be said in
these exact words, "Sit down, you can't go to the
bathroom til we say so." Then we all knew this was
the shit.

First they called The Boys into the secret rooms
down the hallway. In my stoned paranoia I knew
the CAVITY SEARCH was happening but I just didn't
want to think about it. And of course they called
me in last. I only saw one of the Meices as the
woman police officer that looked like John Denver
in a Farrah Faucet wig led me into what would
become the room from hell. I was shaking from
the pot and was nauseated by the thought of this
he/she government bitch touching me. But before
I could get sick the touching began. She sat me
down on the floor and took off my boots. At first
this kind of amused me as I sold shoes when I
wasn't "rocking out." But sitting there stoned, my
bare feet freezing, the humor was missing. Then
she told me to stand up facing the wall. I did, and
immediately she kicked my feet apart, like on
Bareta. Then she dumped out my backpack. My
heart really pounded, I had some codeine which is
legal in Canada in my pack. And I knew it wasn't
legal to bring it back to the U.S., and I had forgotten it was in there. Of course she found it and

asked what it was for, "personal use" I said, feeling
articulate. "1200 tablets?" she asked. She dumped
it all out on the floor and threw the empty bottles
by my shoes. Then I heard one of the Meices say
"Ow! That hurts!" My heart stopped and then
police woman Farrah Denver says to me, "Drop
your pants." My heart fell and my stomach turned.
I wasn't stoned anymore, I was repulsed. With my
pants around my ankles and only my bra on by
this point she calls in back-up. I can't see them. I
am considered dangerous because of the "drugs"
and apparently someone else had a sharp object on
their person. Every sick, hungover, tired tour
muscle in my body was revolted as she ran her
thick leathery hand all over me. Holding back my
smart ass comments I felt her hand head south.
Tightening my stomach I felt it, yes, it was the
front and rear hands-on CAVITY SEARCH!!!! I
started to heave. She pulled away and I turned
toward her and saw that her back up was a group
of 4 men who had been watching her violate me!
And the fucked up part is, it was all legal for her to
do! She was looking out for the American public!
At that moment I knew this was the most fucked up
day of my life, and possibly a curse on the rest of
the tour. I had no way of knowing it was only 3
o'clock and I had the whole fucked up day to live
before me....

When she finally left me to dress in the room I took
a stoned chance and refilled the codeines and put
them in my bag. When I came back into the waiting room I saw the sad rock blobs all sitting in a
row waiting to be allowed into our home country.
They all looked at me with pity, they knew I had
been "searched" in all the wrong places and could
tell I was about to cry. Even thier funky b.o. hugs
didn't help. I needed to purge that she/he from my

private parts right then. They let us go in a long or short while (I still am not sure how long) and we headed back to Seattle.

In Bellingham, we happened to stop at the same gas station as Kill Sybil. They asked why we looked so fucked. I told them and they thought I was making it up, until they looked in my eyes. Then they just said, "yuk!" and climbed back in the van.

The three hour drive went by okay, and never before had home looked so good. We fought to be first out of the vehicle that had caused us so much violation. Like a bad sit-com we fell over each other into the house. The first thing to greet us was the smell of wet, then the sound of running water, then someone yelled, "your faucet exploded!" The day from hell was just greeted by satan. My house was flooded. We just stood there; then I finally cried. Fuck rock. Fuck touring. Fuck leaving my house! The Meices were great and I ladled out my house. By then it was late, 7:30 or so and we just had to take some codeine, smoke a bowl and take a nap. As we all said good napping and were about to find a dry place to curl up and hopefully die for awhile, we heard a choking sound. (Yes, it keeps going!) We all looked into the kitchen that still had enough water on the floor to float plastic boats, and my 22 pound cat projectile vomited on top of the water. We watched the half chewed moist cat food float across the room. We almost laughed but just couldn't. Joe Meice loaded a bowl and we somehow passed out.—*But wait, there's more, remember, we are on tour supporting our record releases*—I wake up to go pee and I hear a voice talking into the answering machine, it's the booking agent from the club Kill Sybil and The Meices are supposed to be playing at that night.

"The show starts in 1/2 an hour! Where are you?
The doors opened at 8! Call me! Tammy, your
band's here, where are you and those Meices?!" I
just start shaking and laughing and woke everyone
up. I put on a fancy dress and Mark Meice tells me
I look "Californian" while he puts on a suit coat,
'cause remember, "it's not how you look, but how
you feel that's important."

Kill Sybil and The Meices finished up that tour, and
over a year later it is still hands down the worst
day of my life.

King Missile

"And at a certain point, Roger would lay down on the piano bench and I'd spray Shit-In-A-Can on him."

KING MISSILE

John Hall (vocals) and Roger (drums) interviewed by Greg at The Casbah in San Diego, CA.

John: We had a night off in New Orleans and we, uh, I don't drink, which means that I have no excuse, Roger was drunk and there were some other people with us as well. So we decided to go to, I don't know, we went around, up and down the French Quarter. I bought some Shit-In-A-Can, because I figured it'd probably come in handy. You know, they have all these stupid novelty things in all the stores....Shit-In-A-Can....O.K., why not. We went to this karaoke club and it was a real yuppy thing and everybody gets drunk and everybody sings songs. So, we worked it out that I would get up there and sing "I Am Woman." And at a certain point, Roger would lay down on the piano bench and I'd spray Shit-In-A-Can, on him, like towards the end of the song. You know, I guess the idea was to sort of disrupt the evening and shock people (laughs). So we did exactly that and I sprayed it all over him and nobody responded at all. Nobody laughed, everybody was just staring. I think that they were catatonically drunk. Like everybody there was just completely, out of their minds drunk. I mean the host didn't even bat an eye, he just kind of pushed us off the stage.

Greg: Did the stuff smell?

John: No, no. It just looked like shit. Like fake shit. And then afterwards we were really upset because we found out that you could video tape and we didn't. Posterity lost. I'm trying to think of any-

thing else that happened on the road. But everything seems to go pretty smoothly for us. There's
actually this guy in San Diego, the few times we've
played. And, uh, he just really loves to kiss me. You
know, and like, each time he tries to get a little
more off of me. I'm not the gay one in the band.

L7

"Donita was
playing with
her pants down
around her
ankles..."

L7

As told by Jennifer Finch and Man Heart (roadie).

This is an L7 tour story from a tour of the United States in 1991. It was in Austin, Texas; L7 has lots of friends there. If L7 has lots of friends there you know you are going to get into a lot of trouble. We roll into town and we are not there ten minutes before there are like fifteen people there to hang out with L7. We played a show at the Cannibal Club; it was a good show; lots of people; fight; all the good stuff. Finch was punching people from stage, and all the good things that go on. Donita was playing with her pants down around her ankles.

We were done, and there's David Deway from CatButt, our friend Cumbala from the Acid Cowgirls, and Danny Flame, the guy who does films for Butthole Surfers hanging out. They hear there's this frat party that we've got to go to, and Austin is this big college town with a great history of jocks vs. the punkers.

All of a sudden we're going to a frat party, which, to me, always sounds like a bad idea from past experience, but everyone says it will be great. They have some weird...like...beach theme at this frat party. It was a Vietnam theme. They have the main room of their frat filled with four inches of water, and everyone is wearing fatigues, and there are palm trees, etc. Of course, there is tons of beer and tons of frat boys, and seventeen of us all show up. We get there at two in the morning and the thing is starting to die down.

So what we're dealing with is seventeen people who still want to get a keg, and three frat boys standing between us and the keg. We have this really great idea that what is going to happen is Cathy Cowgirl,with some of the gals in L7, is going to distract the frat boys. Then I (Finch), and I don't even drink but I came up with the scheme, I am going to roll the keg off the second story. Other people downstairs are going to grab the keg and throw it in the van, and then we would all evacuate. So everything goes really fine, everyone is dancing, the frat boys are distracted. We roll the keg off, but the two people who were supposed to catch it, forgot.

The keg hits the ground, the frat boys are really distracted, and the evacuation call is made. We all start running like in four inches of water to get out of this frat party. We jump in the van but we notice Cathy Cowgirl is missing. So it's a frat house, right? So we all start assuming that she is getting gang banged in one of the rooms by like fifteen frat guys. So here we are with the keg, yelling back and forth with the three guys who were responsible for the keg, trying to get it back.

While this is going on a couple of us are running up and down through the entire frat yelling, "Cathy! Cathy! Cathy!!!" She is nowhere around. We all get back in the van, deciding that Cathy went to get a Big Gulp or something. All of a sudden David Deway is missing from CatButt; simultaneously my shoes are missing. Now we're looking everywhere for David Deway, thinking he is being gang raped by fifteen frat guys. So we're banging up and down the halls. We finally find him in the basement, which is in three feet of water. He is laying with his nose just above the water line with one of my shoes floating on his chest. When his chest expanded it would catch the shoe, and when he'd breath out the shoe would start to float away, then he'd catch it again with his stomach. We finally load him into the van, and everyone is soaking wet, we had to do some rolls with the frat boys at the end.

We take the keg to Cumbala's second story apartment and put it out on his porch. He has been having problems with his landlady who lives downstairs to begin with. She is up there at four in the morning, banging on the door telling us to be quiet. He is trying to be diplomatic, but everyone is really drunk.

We wake up in the morning, its like 6:30 am. The landlady bangs on the door again because the keg had spilt over, all the beer had dripped off of the balcony and filled her bird bath. And that's pretty much the end of the story.

The side note to the story is that the guys from the Hickoids were supposed to go on tour and leave at 9:00 am that morning. But Jeff Smith was partying with us, and passed out on the floor. While we are cleaning out the bird bath, the land lady is yelling at us, frat boys are circling the neighborhood, and the Hickoid van pulls up. They walk up, pick up Jeff, and carry him Jesus style out into their van, where they have thrown an entire drawer of his clothing for the trip. And they went on tour; and then they broke up somewhere in Southern California.

Luscious Jackson

"In celebration
of Blackie's
birthday, we all
popped No-Doz
and went cow
tipping."

LUSCIOUS JACKSON

San Francisco to Oregon

(Vivian has flown ahead to meet her parents in Portland)

Dear Viv...

Miss you already. Life in the van is not quite the same without you. We each have our own bench seat.

Tonight you missed out on Dairy Queen and double cappuccinos in the front seat (hence this letter). We're driving through the valley where its 100 degrees at night. The bug to windshield ratio works out to be about 100 deaths per minute. The sound track is pure classic rock, Frampton is alive once again.

Today we talked on the radio and since you weren't there, no one heard you. In your absence, however, we made sure to make use of the words: plethora, myriad and cornucopia.

Re: The van break in. The criminal profile has been determined by the items stolen, which follow: 1 Led Zeppelin tape (Physical Graffiti), pimple cream, James Smalley's *A Thousand Acres*, your roadie light, two packs of grape pez, and Mike's fanny pack...Jill's leather boot collection remained untouched. Draw your own conclusions.

We are headed toward Weed, CA where we will be purchasing corduroy caps emblazoned with the word "Weed." We had yet another backseat discussion about anal sex techniques. Too bad you missed out, but the word "fluted" did not come up this time around.

How was your plane ride after the stressful
AM...did you eat the eggs? Per usual, Mike did.

Did you encounter any more Vivian devotees on the
flight? Speaking of fans...here are some of post-
show comments that came our way: 3 teens told us
they listened to only our record for 8 hours straight
while on ecstasy, a smashed English girl asked Jill
"Have you fooked any of the members of Urge
Overkill yet?", Sixties SF casualty, Bob, compared us
unfavorably to Etta James and Janis Joplin, a suave
bolla Bucky Pope (former Tar Baby, current Cold
Cock Trio) appeared in a tuxedo and said nice
things. As always Pat "Mangina" Carpenter
showed up.

New: Goat Oatie Kato fessed up to copping UO
Nash Kato's name. Bob Mack was physically re-
moved from the night club (sans shirt). Chryssie
Hinde was spotted with merch-king Tommy by the
T-shirt stand. Shockingly, the Mullet turnout at
our Bay Area shows was pitiful.

Well Viv...the road to Weed is long and painful,
and we keep seeing smudgy signs for leaping deer.

xoxo Luscious Jackson

P.S. Jill's twelve pack of suntan knee-highs are still
AWOL.

Seattle to Denver

(Urge has flown to San Diego to do the X-fest and
will meet us in Denver)

Dear Boys...

A note from Stinker's truck-stop: Since you all
were forced to miss the glamour of Idaho, let us re-
cap it for you.

Mostly there's an intense lack of color in this state;
the people, food and land are a basic beige. The
official state scent seems to be manure (Gabby says
"egg farts"). Yesterday's highlight was a gas station milkshake machine. Last night a hostile red-
neck called our beloved Mike a long-haired freak
and threatened us when we asked for a gas receipt.
As usual, we missed our projected destination by
200 miles and 2 hours.

Forced to seek shelter, we were thrilled to find that
the Boise airport-area swinger scene is as hot as
they say! Upon exiting the bathroom of our hotel
"spa," Jill surprised two hideous blonde hot-tub
patrons who grinned maniacally through clenched
teeth. We sampled the glorious complimentary
continental breakfast (featuring the Idaho staple
"Creamora") but made sure to leave room for
Stinker's world-famous potato salad. As we gaze
upon the uneventful beige landscape, our dreams
of farm-life shatter.

In celebration of Blackie's birthday, we all popped
No-Doz and went cowtipping.

While sleeping in a quasi-69 position (due to lack of
space), Jill and Gabby tried to pass gas simultaneously, but failed over and over again. We realized you can't always get what you want.

F.Y.I: The toilet at the "Sod Buster" restaurant lets
out a strange high-pitched moan when you flush it
and there are 26 varieties of beef jerky at Mr. Gas.

xoxo Luscious Jackson

Denver to Minneapolis
(We long for a coast)

Dear God,

it's us Luscious,

Life on the road is getting monotonous...we've seen a million places and we've rocked them all.

While driving along staring boredly out the window at livestock, we were feeling sort of sorry for cows and their mundane lives. Then we thought a little more about a cow's life: they know exactly when they will be fed, milked and put to sleep in their cozy barns. Viv pointed out that knowing when and where we would be fondled every day and where our next meal would come from would be quite luxurious.

Today we entered a new word into the Luscious Jackson dictionary: Gabby coined the phrase "Pyew, huh?" to describe the scent of the Mid-west. We get more and more delirious with each passing field...our minds are wound tight like balls of hay...we wonder nightly why the restaurant vegetables of choice in the rolling farmlands of Nebraska are powdered mashed potatoes, wilted Iceberg lettuce and canned peas. Never in our lives did we anticipate that someday we'd have a burning desire to reach Minneapolis.

So God, we're offering you a deal: We'll keep a stiff upper lip for the next fourteen hour drive, we won't even mention the polyester sheets and cinder block walls in the Motel 6s, just help us find an okay radio station for the hours ahead and some leafy greens in Minneapolis and we'll call it even...

xoxo Luscious Jackson

Mary's Danish

"There is nothing like a bad martini to blot the senses."

MARY'S DANISH

As told by Julie Ritter

THREE FOR THE ROAD

October 1992

Hutch, James and I went to what I think was called the Alibi Room tonight for martinis. There we met 2 genial coeds, one of whom offered to take us off-roading the next day. Hutch went, while I declined the invitation, thinking how a social engagement made over cheap martinis in the wrong shaped glass seemed to bode ill. Hutch said he had a really good time, though we kept forgetting our coed's name. Later, we had trouble recollecting what the bar was called, and still today, we cannot reconcile the episode with the city in which it took place. It leads me to only one conclusion. There is nothing like a bad martini to blot the senses.

November 1992

Our cab ride today from New Jersey to New York eclipsed all previous cab rides. This topped the guy in Columbus who drove head on into the median for gasoline and chocolate. This was even more brilliant than the time the guy drives 3 miles out of our way to show us the outside of his house and ask us if we wanted to go in and smoke a joint. This cabbie today came 45 minutes after we called, backed up into another car, demolishing it before we even left the hotel, got us lost going through the Holland Tunnel, and was finally pulled over by the cops once we got into Manhattan. He kept saying how it wasn't his day. The cop looked into the back seat to ask us where we were headed. When Mario, our driver, answered him, the cop barked "Shut the fuck up." It was New York's finest at its finest. I'd say it was even better than the 80 dollar cab fare to the movies in Rhode Island, and the Philly driver who took us to the gig and never once faltered while doing his best John Wayne.

March 1993

As the sun set this evening, we were forced to examine the dubious prospect of finding health food in Fresno. I corralled those yearnings to explore alternative dinner possibilities, swearing up and down that I had found a vegetarian restaurant that was open late. An hour and a half later, James and Gretchen displayed unprecedented discipline when we arrived to find the proprietress of said restaurant in a flooded kitchen. We dined instead at Safeway and cursed our bad luck as we winded our way back to the hotel through the dusky Fresno streets.

Melvins

"...it was
obviously just a
local who had,
'had enough of
this fucking
punk rock
shit.'"

MELVINS

Buzz (guitar, vocals) and Dave (drums) were interviewed by Greg.

Buzz: We've been around a long time, our first U. S. tour was in 1986, the summer of '86.

We had one single out, and were playing the kind of music that we're playin' now. The tour was not going real well, needless to say, the only thing that saved our butts was that we were opening for this band called RKL. They were a lot more established than us. We rolled into Florida. Florida at that time was inhabited by a lot of skinheads. We had ultra, you know, long, long hair and beards; that's basically what it amounted to. These skinheads were like some of the biggest dummies I've ever been around; I mean they fucked with us non stop on that tour. RKL's drummer used to be a skinhead, and that was the only thing that saved us...'cos they liked us. At a lot of the shows we'd show up and the promoters, who happened to be skinheads, would just say, "You guys aren't playing." And RKL would say, "Yes they are playing, or we're not playing." So that happened and a lot of it amounted to us opening shows. We had driven from the Seattle area; we were in Florida, and Florida was skinhead haven. They all hated us. In Tampa (FL) we opened a bill with four other local bands and RKL. We had to open the bill or else we couldn't play (laughs). And these were shit bands. Anyway, Vince was the promoter's name. Vince was very, very, very dumb. This was the summer of '86, and he was a dumb, racist skinhead. As far as they were concerned, we were hippies, you know, and that was it. Vince invites us back to his house and it was in this black neighborhood.

Greg: A skinhead lives in a black neighborhood?

Buzz: Yeah, a house of skins. Now, before we showed up, one of Vince's buddies was talkin' to me about music. I was talking about how I like Jimi Hendrix and he goes, "Well there's one thing I don't like about Hendrix." And I was like, "What?" "Well he's black."

That kind of set the mood for the whole thing. I was just like, "Jesus Christ...Get me outta here!" So we roll into Vince's house. The first thing I notice when we get there is this giant burned cross...KKK, you know? And two giant swastikas painted on...like twin swastikas painted on both sides of the front door and the walls of the house. It was one of the most terrifying nights I've ever spent. Of course they wouldn't let the "hippies" sleep in the house or anything like that. The house was demo'd anyway, completely destroyed. So we spent the night out-side. They said that the "niggers" had been giving them a lot of trouble and they couldn't figure out why. I was like, guys, figure it out. So we slept out in front of the house all night. Recently a couple of car loads of black..."niggers" as they called 'em, had driven by, shooting into their house. I over-heard one of them saying, "The good thing about having their van out there man, is that any bullets will have to go through it before they get to the house." We didn't have any money, anything to do; we stayed there because we had nowhere to go. Thinking back, we should have just taken off, but we didn't really want to get too far away from RKL because we felt like they were the only people that could keep us alive. So that was one of the most horrifying nights I've ever spent, and we got the

HELL outta there the next day.

On this last tour that we just did, we rolled into Lawrence, KS; we were supposed to play at the Outhouse. We had heard about this place for a long long time, but this was the first time we'd ever been there; we always missed the center of the U.S. on our tours. Last Fall was the first time we'd actually toured in the center of the U.S. So we roll into town; they have toll roads in the Midwest and on the East Coast, stupidest things I've ever seen. There will be a toll booth in the middle of nowhere, no bridge or anything; you just stop and pay a toll. So we stopped at a toll booth and asked the guy, "Hey can you direct us to..." and he goes, "Oh, you guys are going to the Outhouse." We go, "Yeah, yeah you're right." So it was a pretty well known place in town. He gives us directions to this club, and it's like six in the afternoon. We're getting there plenty early for sound check, or whatever. We're driving in the middle of this corn field, literally, and that's what we had always heard. We're on this flat, dirt road, and we just drive, and drive, and drive. Finally, we see this blue building out in the middle of this corn field, sure enough. So we pull up to the gate and there's a guy there that tells us, "Yeah man, it will be cool. Don't worry, don't worry." And we were all, "What, what the hell?" So we're looking around to see what's going on and all of a sudden we see all these cops in there. Just a bunch of cop cars; we look real close and there's a tow truck, with this big four wheel drive truck up on the back of it, getting ready to drive off. The front of the truck is plowed, all crushed in, it's wrecked. So we idle into the parking lot and this guy from the club comes up and says, "Jesus Christ, some red-neck just tried to kill us." Then we noticed that there was a giant hole in

the front of the building. It was really obvious that
this truck, well, that someone had plowed a truck
straight through the club, right through the front
door wall, and he took the wall with him. So we
were like, "Goddamn! What happened?" And the
promoter is this little kid and he tells us, "Man, this
red-neck pulled into the parking lot and he gets
out of his truck, and starts yelling, 'Which one of
you faggots wants to fight me?' He was just all
tanked up and he was wearing a pair of boots and
his underwear, and that was it. And he started
going, 'Which one of you faggots wants to fight
me, you wierdos!' and stuff like that, and I guess he
was threatening all these people. And they were
just all, 'Man just leave us alone, just get out of
here,' you know?" He was saying all this stuff about
wierdos and it was obviously just a local who had,
"had enough of this fucking punk rock shit out
here." Then he got in his truck and started doing
all these doughnuts and stuff in the parking lot,
and people were standing out there. All of a sudden
he starts chasing people with his truck, trying to
hit them, literally trying to kill people. He was
trying to run them over. Then he goes after the
promoter whose dodging around and the guy is
chasing him in his truck. He said "I was running as
fast as I could" and he ran through the front door
of the club and dove behind this thing. And the
guy in the truck just plowed. Just followed him
right through into the club. He didn't touch his
brakes, or anything; just bammo, right through
this cinder block building. He took out a good
twelve feet of wall. He ended up embedded into the
building, and uh, by the time we got there it was
all over; the cops took him away. The promoter was
worried that he'd probably get out and bring some
of his red-neck buddies back to the club that night.

(Laughs). We were like, "Jesus Christ!" We could just see visions of these red-necks with shotguns coming back saying (in a mock red-neck accent) "BillyBob got in trouble with them fags down there...and we're going to go get some of them."

DALE THE DRUMMER WALKS INTO THE VAN

Buzz: We're doing a tour stories interview.

Dale: Cool.

Greg: So did you guys play that night?

Buzz: Yeah, so anyway, the show goes on. We played and it was cool! It was cool! It was a good enthusiastic show. We got to about our last song and the promoter comes running up to the stage; this place is pretty full, packed, you know, pretty good crowd, and the promoter says, "You guys gotta stop, you gotta stop!" We say, "OK, fine." We stopped and they were saying something about a fight outside. So we go outside and there's this giant pool of blood with this guy laying in it. This ambulance driver is testing his feet to see if he could feel anything. He was beaten so badly that they had to take him away on a back board. Apparently, some neighboring skinhead type people or something had come to the show that night and just pounded the shit out of this guy. We just loaded our shit and said, "Let's just get out of here man!"

Dale: Yeah, that whole day was just bad news.

Buzz: One cool thing about this was that someone told us about these black guys in the neighborhood, or the area, who had started shaving their heads and became black skinheads. They started beating the shit out of any white skinheads that they found. We thought that was really cool.

Naked Raygun

"So he orders his fucking stromboli. It literally took two-and-a-half hours to make this stromboli."

NAKED RAYGUN

Pierre Kezdy was interviewed by Greg Jacobs at the Casbah in San Diego, CA

Pierre: This is when John (Haggerty) had just quit Naked Raygun, so we had a new guitar player, Bill Stevens. Our regular roadie couldn't make it, so I got this marine friend of mine to do it. He's a total marine! We had to do some special gig in New York. The roadie and Bill drove out with the van. We all, the rest of us (in the band) flew out. (After the show) everybody else except me, the roadie and Bill Stevens drove back. We figured, "Ah fuck you know, New York to Chicago, 17 hours, we'll just go right through." So we get out of New York, its about 5:00, and the roadie says, "I gotta get something to eat, I'm fuckin' hungry." I go no, let's just keep driving. And he has to stop at a gas station in "podunk" Pennsylvania. And this place was ancient, it was from the 1930s. He looks through the dusty old menu and he sees stromboli on there. He has to have a stromboli. So he orders his fuckin' stromboli. It literally took two-and-a-half hours to make this stromboli. We just sat in this fuckin' gas station and they kept saying: "Oh, its coming, its coming." Two-and-a-half hours at this gas station for this stromboli. So finally we got back on the road, we kept driving and we got tired, so we pull over at a hotel.The next morning we get out, get right on the Ohio State Turnpike and I'm driving the van. All of a sudden you just hear this explosion, and smoke starts pouring through the dash. White smoke starts pouring through the dash, and I thought, "White smoke...it must be a radiator

hose." So I pull over to the side of the road. We pile
out of the van. And the smoke is starting to come
out the front now. We were thinking, "Shit, a little
radiator hose?" And then we thought "Oh jeez, I
hope its not on fire!" All three of us look down
below the van and as soon as we looked down
flames shoot out from underneath the van. All
these semi's pull over; they've got there fire extin-
guishers out, they couldn't put it out. We start
hauling our gear out, throwing it down the ditch,
so we had drums rolling down the ditch, amps
rolling down the ditch. We were trying to get
everything out. Now the smoke is turning black,
the flames are up in front. We were all trying to
pull all of our personal shit out of there but the
smoke got too bad, and the big amps were still in
there. I said, "Fuck it, just let it burn." The marine
guy says "Oh no, we've gotta go in and get it." He
fuckin' goes in there. So I figured if he's going in
there, I'm going in there too. Luckily the wind
direction changed towards the front of the van, we
got the amps out. When the two amps were out
flames started shooting out the back. The guitar
player says, "I left my leather jacket in there." What
does the marine do? He says, "I'll go get it." Fucking
flames were shooting out of the van, he jumps in
there, grabs the leather jacket and comes out
totally unscathed. By then the fire department
showed up and they just let the thing burn. The
fuel line was feeding the fire. It burned to a crisp.
Then I called Jeff (Pezzati the singer), he had already gotten back and he was at work. He had all
the insurance papers and stuff. I said, " Jeff guess
what?" He said, "what?" I said, "The van burned!"
And he goes, "just get it fixed and drive back," you
know," put it on your credit card or something."
And I said, "No you don't understand, the van is

toast!" He goes, "Well stay over night somewhere and get it fixed and come back." I said "You don't understand; the van is fucking gone!" There was literally nothing, all the tires burned, everything burned. It was just a metal hull sitting on the highway. It took Jeff 5 minutes to realize that the van was gone. Plus, we had 1000 t-shirts that were not insured, so we lost about $5000 in shirts. That was pretty hairy!

Greg: How did you guys get home?

Pierre: It was weird, they had the whole tollway closed off, traffic was piled up for miles. It was about an hour before the van burned down. The State Troopers drove me to the Toledo airport and arranged for me to get a van somewhere. We got a van, and some other guy with a pick up truck in the meanwhile had taken our gear off the highway for us. We gave him $25 or $50, whatever. Yeah, so it turned out alright except for losing those shirts. It was pretty fuckin' hairy though!

Overwhelming Colorfast

"We made a bike ramp and took a bunch of toilet paper, doused it with lighter fluid and lit it on fire."

OVERWHELMING COLORFAST

Bob was interviewed by Greg Jacobs.

Bob: We were touring with the Treepeople through the Mid-West and played this club. The bartender threw a big barbeque for us and everything was great. It was a really cool show and everybody was drinking Jagermeister and, uh, there may have been some psychedelics passed around, I 'm not sure. But after the show was over, the club cleared out, we locked the doors and set some plywood up, from the end of the stage down onto the floor of the club. Then we made a bike ramp and took a bunch of toilet paper, doused it with lighter fluid and lit it on fire. Then we took turns jumping over it on a mountain bike, until the manager from the Treepeople ran the bike into the wall and bent the forks in. So, that was about after 10 people had taken turns..."Flaming Bike!" And, the bartender let us have full run of the bar and we came up with a really heinous drink that night, called "The Flaming Bike!" I don't think anybody knows what the hell was in it exactly, but it went down pretty smooth!

Popdefect

"He then tells the three of us, plus a friend who is along for the ride, to get down on our knees..."

POPDEFECT

We were driving up north from Los Angeles, I guess
it was to San Francisco. No, actually it was all the
way up to Seattle. We pull out of a gas station at
about two o'clock in the morning, somewhere in
the middle of the big San Joaquin Valley, and this
cop pulls us over. I couldn't think of any reason
why we had been stopped, but we pulled over. All
of a sudden the police officer tells everyone to put
their hands outside the windows and get out of the
driver's side of the car. He then tells the three of
us, plus a friend who is along for the trip, to get
down on our knees. The cops had their guns
drawn and asked us if there was anyone being held
against his will. We all said, ahh...yeah, none of us
want to be here at this point in time.

So they take Al, the guitar player, over to search
the van, and the cop has his gun on him the whole
time. The other cop is still got his gun drawn as
well, holding it on the rest of us. Of course we
have an old van and the locks don't work, so Al has
to reach inside the van in a weird way to unlock it.
As he is doing this Al is explaining to the officer
exactly what he is doing, and he can hear the
officer pull the hammer back on the gun. They
finally search the van, taking care of that sort of
business, and then explain why they had pulled us
over. Apparently, a trucker had radioed in that he
had seen someone in the van frantically pointing a
hand at the word "HELP," which I had painted on
the van on a hot summer day in Dallas a few
months earlier. The trucker imagined that he'd
seen someone pointing at this sign and called it in.

So the police had been after us.

We eventually get back on the road, and we are driving away, and in no more than five minutes we catch up to these two tractor trailer trucks. And these two semi's block the road, they take up both lanes. Then all of a sudden they start slowing down...50...40...30...20 miles per hour. We start thinking, oh great, vigilantes. They think the cops are fucked and they're going to pull us out and start shooting or something. We finally got enough room to get by and got away, but it was more than a pretty eerie feeling there for a couple of miles. (1987)

Another time we had been on tour for about two months. We came back to L.A. and played the Southland for a couple of weeks and we were about to go out again for a couple of months. We were still booking our own tours at this point and Al had somehow hooked up with this guy from Pensacola, Florida who was a blind wrestler. He mainly handled wrestling events, but he also did rock shows. He was going to set up the first leg of the tour, I think it was five dates, between New Orleans and Pensacola. We didn't have anything before New Orleans. We just drove straight from L.A. to New Orleans.

In the meantime, this promoter, wrestler guy had called us, obviously unaware that it took forty-eight hours to drive from L.A. to New Orleans, and said that the show was cancelled. So we finally get a hold of him while in New Orleans, he had been out on tour doing the wrestling thing. He says, "Yeah...yeah the show in New Orleans was can-celled, but come to Pensacola, I've got something for you there." So we got drunk in New Orleans that night, slept in the van, and drove out to

Pensacola the next day. We get out there, show up at the club, and they had never heard of us. We are saying, "What the fuck?"

We finally get a hold of the promoter and he says, "Sorry...sorry it fell through, but go back to New Orleans. I got something for out there at Tulane, the college." We gave a hesitant, "Okay," and went back out to New Orleans. Once again, there is no show. He again says to go back to Pensacola. By this time we have given up on the Blind Wrestler, but we return to Pensacola anyway. We didn't have anywhere else to go. We never even met the Blind Wrestler Man. That was an evil beginning to the second leg of our tour. Don't ever book a tour with a blind wrestler. (1988)

Once we were coming back from Chicago, going to Seattle by way of Minnesota. It was extremely cold out. Nick, a friend Paul and I were playing cards in the back of the van, drinking whiskey. Al was driving when it started to drizzle just a little bit. Two minutes later the van starts to slide back and forth. So I ask Al if in fact that was the case. As soon as he finished saying, "yeah...I think it might be," we start doing 360s at sixty miles per hour, right down the middle of the freeway. It was really incredible because nobody was panicking, there was no screaming. We sat there looking at each other, cards still in hand, thinking "huh...this is interesting." Just before we slide off the road, Al delivers a coy, "I'm sorry."

Fortunately, the meridian between the freeway was relatively level, so we slid to a circling halt. No one was hurt, but all the cards had been crushed in our fists. There was no damage to the van until I put my hand through the tail light, trying to push it back onto the freeway. We pulled off at the next exit and decided to splurge and stay in a hotel, only the second time we had ever done that. (1990)

Rocket from the Crypt

"...and we
rubbed his butt
on the hardwood
floor until he
got splinters in
his butt."

ROCKET FROM THE CRYPT

John Reis (vocals, guitar) interveiwed by Greg.

John: Something that happened to Rocket From The Crypt... We were out for about a month and a half, which is not a real long time, but it was our first tour in Fall of 1991. And you know how it gets, everyone's away from their girlfriends and so forth.

And it's the time when a growing boy/man comes to grips with his loneliness. Someone in the band decided that it would be a good idea to masturbate while the other members of the band drove and pioneered our vehicle through the countryside. And his actions weren't appreciated by the other band members. Everyone got very pissed off. I, for one, got very mad just for the fact that he was looking at the back of my head while he was doing this. So we gave him names such as "Spanky," and "Wacker" and so forth.

Then all throughout the rest of the tour, he lived a life of hell, until the climax was probably...the literal climax was when we duct taped him up, and kind of got him naked and rubbed his bare butt on (there were hardwood floors in the van we rented); we rubbed his butt on the hardwood floors until he got splinters in his butt. And then we just beat the shit out of him, literally, and took his money. And we filmed it! And that's what you get for masturbating.

Greg: You filmed it?

John: Yeah! It's all on video. We taped him to the
ground so that he couldn't move, and that's what
happened. So, it's really nothing that bad.....but......

Screaming Sirens

"When we got
off stage,
the guys from
Supertramp gave
us coke and
bought us
drinks..."

SCREAMING SIRENS

Opening for Supertramp in St. Louis, Missouri
By Pleasant Gehman

This event took place in 1985 or 1986, when the
Screaming Sirens, my insane all-girl liquor soaked
"cow punk" band was in the midst of it's second US
tour, supporting our first album, "Fiesta!"

It all started in Nashville. Friends of ours came
from all over Tennessee (and we had quite a few
friends in that state, at the time) to see us play our
last gig in that area, at Rooster's. It was our bassist
Laura's birthday – the eve of her birthday. At
midnight we were going to celebrate. We were on
the bill with some band called something about
Science, and though they remained unknown, at
that point, they had a financial backer, a
humongous, air conditioned/heated tour bus with
beds and a refrigerator, a driver, and full road
crew. We were living like road pigs, staying at
people's houses on the floor, no showers, no heat in
our van (it was the middle of November) shitty
money at our gigs. We got real drunk with the
other band – they were cute boys – and they all
new it was Laura's birthday, so they were partying
us down. I went outside to get some air, and there,
in the weeds leaning against the side of the club,
was this freshly-dug up gravestone from the nine-
teen hundreds, the headstone of a girl who died at
the age of twenty-four (the age Laura was turning)
on the day Laura was born! What better present? I
got a roadie and with the help of like, five other
people (the stone was so big and heavy) we loaded

it onto a dolly and brought it up to the dressing room on the elevator.

Instead of the anticipated reaction of laughter, and cries of "no way!" Laura was completely terrified. She flipped out.

"Get that fucking thing out of here right now," she said, her voice trembling.

We thought it was forgotten, but the headstone put a curse on the whole next day. That night, after the show partying at a restaurant with the other band, Laura somehow left her purse, with all her ID and all her money in the parking lot of the restaurant. When we went back to look for it, it was gone. Then, she and I had the late-night driving shift – we were going to St. Louis – and it began to pour so hard it was difficult to see out the windshield. We were dead tired, and had no speed - there wasn't even anywhere to get coffee, because nowhere was open, and it was freezing. Finally, three and a half hours later, we got to an open convenience mart, only to discover we'd gone that whole distance in the wrong direction.

Getting back on course, we rolled through Kentucky, trying to make good time because we had a show that night. Instead, we got pulled over for speeding. Laura, of course, was driving and she had no ID because her purse was lost. Not only that, the red-neck cop was horrified because she had on a vintage, falling apart sealskin coat and men's long underwear, and I was sitting there in my stage clothes (ripped up petticoats, fishnets, a handcuff belt, corset and a parka), and we both had last night's makeup on. Not a pretty picture.

She explained to the cop about her purse, and he went through the whole scene of calling LA to see if

we were hardened criminals or something — he got
her DOB, so it was obvious it was her birthday, we
told him WHY we were speeding (on a deserted
country road at seven AM) and he didn't care. He
wrote us a huge ticket, anyway.

We finally got to St. Louis, and looked for a post
office so we could spend our earnings back home.
The way things were going, the thought of having
almost $2,000.00 worth of cash was frightening.
Besides, the gig tonight was really one of the best-
paying shows on the tour. So we got out money
orders, and sent the cash back to LA, keeping one
day's per diem per girl (we got $10.00 a day, each.
Shit pay even for back then!) We got lost, of-course,
on the way to the club, but when we finally got
there, it was like "Screaming WHO?" They'd fired
the booking agent about a month ago, cancelled all
his bookings, and no one bothered to tell us. Our
next gig was three days away — and we had like
sixty dollars between seven people, plus whatever
personal money we had stashed, which, in
everyone's case wasn't more than five or ten bucks.
And Laura, of course, had zilch. We'd just gotten
rid of the entire band fund, too. We were sitting in
the parking lot all afternoon, freezing. We'd
pleaded about playing, even for tips, but the new
booking agent didn't want to go through the
hassle. It started to snow. The house band was
booked there to play five top forty sets that night.
They found out we were girls and spied on our van.
We offered them some pot; it was all we had, and
in our predicament, we needed some sedation. They
retaliated by smuggling beers and popcorn out
from the club. Finally, they told us that
Supertramp was playing at some coliseum down
the street, and the after-party was at the club here.

They invited us to play a short set on their equipment and said they'd get it ok'd. We had a dismal dinner at an Italian low-budget place that sucked, then went to the club. It was packed with millions of people. The house band was being really nice – getting us pitchers of beer, and everyone was singing "Happy Birthday" to Laura. We played a wild little set and the place went crazy. One of the house band guys explained our predicament on stage and people were sending trays of shots up to the stage and throwing money and stuff. Then, the entire club sang "Happy Birthday" to Laura, and when we got offstage, the guys from Supertramp gave us coke and bought us rounds of drinks and then went on. So we opened for Supertramp. By the end of the night, someone had gotten in tough with the promoter in Kansas City, and he was overjoyed we'd be there a day early and arranged for a free place for us to stay, so our luck turned around. But just like the old cartoon, Laura still shrieks, "Happy Birthday! Oh, NO PLEASE...NOT HAPPY BIRTHDAY! ANYTHING BUT HAPPY BIRTH-DAY!

Skin Yard

"Our drummer threatened to call his mom, get a plane ticket and fly back home..."

SKIN YARD

Interviewed by Greg Jacobs over the phone with
Daniel House (bass).

Daniel: Well I guess the best overall tour story that
comes to mind is "The Tour From Hell" as Skin Yard
collectively refers to it. It was the tour for the
"Hollowed Ground" LP, which is our second LP that
came out in, oh lord, in '87. We had Bulging Eye
booking us, and I am convinced to this day that the
people that booked the tour had never themselves
even been on tour. They essentially booked us on
this tour that had us zig-zagging all over the country. We were doing just insane, ridiculous drives
for, like, $100 a night. A prime example: we had a
Thursday night in Athens, GA; they booked us
Friday in North Carolina, which was a 14 hour
drive north. Then Saturday night they sent us to
Gainesville, FL, which was a 17 hour drive south.
So, basically we had to drive 14 hours north, and 17
hours south, for $100 on a Friday night. After the
gig we had to turn around and head straight back.
The van, itself, was a complete piece of shit and
was probably breaking down about every 500
miles. I think the first place it broke down was in
San Luis Obisbo, CA; we blew an oil gasket. We
made it to Tucson, AZ where we took the heads off
and put in these new gaskets. The auto parts place
actually gave us the wrong gaskets, so we spent a
day and a half doing the work. Then we started up
the engine and oil went spewing everywhere. So
we had to take it all a part again.
During the 14 hour/17hour drive, on the way back

to Florida we broke down in Savannah, GA and spent about six hours under the hood trying desperately to get the car to work so that we could make our gig, which we didn't. Keep in mind, that when we were in Athens, GA we were about three hours away from our Florida gig. Is this very interesting? It seems really boring.

Greg: Yeah, yeah. I can't believe Bulging Eye.

Daniel: It was Bulging Eye. That tour we grossed $3300.00. That was our total gross take from shows. And, uh, Bulging Eye tried to bill us a full $1000.00 for their efforts, basically a full third of our entire gross. We gave them part of it; I think we gave them $700.00, and ended up telling them to eat shit. There were a couple of shows, like that one in North Carolina, where we called and said we wanted to cancel. This is ridiculous. Michelle (from Bulging Eye) ended up screaming at the top of her lungs at me over the phone for about 20 minutes telling us what a bunch of shitheads we were and how it just made Bulging Eye look really bad to have bands cancel the night before the show and all this business, you know? We finally did get to the show and there was no promotion for it anyways. It was just ridiculous. We had $100 nights and we zig-zagged all over the placefor them. Plus, in the midst of all this our drummer was pissed off because he was kind of spoiled and wanted to be making more money than we were making. We basically weren't even making enough money to get per diems on most of the days. So in the middle of it, he threatened to call his mom, get a plane ticket and fly back home if he didn't start seeing some money from the tour. At that point we were up around Rhode Island and we had a friend, Billy Atwell who used to be in the Rhythm Pigs and also the Inbreads. He was a huge fan, we were staying at his house and we jammed with him one day when Scott was doing all this threatening. Billy played every single song perfectly, like better than Scott had the entire tour. After that incident, Scott never once mentioned anything, but he was pretty pissed off at us. We, basically, got back from tour, amazing that we even made it back, and we finished recording the album. That was "Fist Sized Chunks." We basically finished recording the album and kicked Scott out of the band, and broke up for about a year. Basically broke up until the record finally came out. That was the "Tour From Hell!" That was literally the tour that broke us up. It was utterly disheartening, it was so completely miserable. Oh, yeah, actually, to even make matters worse, my son was born literally two weeks before the tour started. So I left on tour with a two week old baby son and when I got back he was two months old. It was awful. It was just utterly miserable. I remember at one point, walking through the streets of Washington, DC just utterly miserable, hating life, hating the tour, hating everybody in the van, hating our booking agent, hating our roadie, missing my wife and son, and I remember just walking through the drizzly rain of Washington, DC just crying. Kind of getting away from everybody cos I didn't want to have everybody see me breaking apart...... (laughs) ....It was awful.

Superchunk

"Four guitars
fell out. Two
of them were
yours."

SUPERCHUNK

By Mac

This happened on our first tour, in the Summer of 1990 with Geek and Seaweed. There were about fifteen of us driving around in all these different vehicles; it was mostly an East Coast tour and a little of the Midwest. We were driving from Pittsburgh to Flint, Michigan. Pittsburgh had been a pretty empty show, and we were looking forward to Flint being pretty much the same.

Anyway, it's a really long drive, and we've got a couple of vans, a car, and a truck with one of those camper tops on the back That's what all the equipment was in. So all of the vehicles get there except the truck, and they're really late. So we're waiting outside of this theater where we're going to be playing; it's an abandoned theater. I think it's called the Capitol Theater. It was in that movie *Roger & Me*, actually. It's a totally abandoned theater; the promoter just had the key to the front door and he's like, "Okay you guys just set up in the lobby," that's where they had the P.A. In the big room I guess they had shows with Styx and bands like that, but we were playing in the lobby. We were supposed to sleep there, too, and the theater was supposed to be haunted or something.

So we're all waiting outside for the stuff to get there. The truck pulls up, and Derrick, the guy who was driving the truck, walks up and he looks really bummed out. And he says, "Well, somewhere along the way the back door of the truck came open and four guitars fell out." Then he looked at me. "Two of them were yours."

Those were my only two guitars. We didn't know
what to do. We were calling the police station in
Pittsburgh, calling all over the place. Finally, we
called some station there, and it turns out that
someone had turned them in. The guitars had
fallen out as they were pulling out of a music store
that morning! And someone turned in all four
guitars. A friend of ours, Brian, drove them up the
next day and met us in Toledo. So we got them
back. But for a couple hours there everyone was
bummed out. The show at the theater though,
turned out to be the most fun show of the tour. It
cost like two dollars to get in, but no one was
paying it. Flint is a totally depressed town,
everything's boarded up, no one's walking around.
So a bunch of people came to the show and stood
outside until we made it free to get in! All everyone
does in Flint is drink, which is what we ended up
doing as well, and it turned into a big water fight.
But it was a fun show, and we slept in the haunted
theater.

Supersuckers

"...and Bolton
was bleeding all
over the place,
and laughing
because he
couldn't believe
they were so mad
at him as to
kick his ass
twice!"

SUPERSUCKERS

There is this time we were playing in Cincinnati
with the Reverend Horton Heat, at this big place
called Bogart's. We played that show and the
Reverend had a bunch of liquor and stuff back
stage and we got pretty hammered. See, I heard
this story kind of second hand because I got too
drunk and passed out and slept in the van, but our
guitar player Dan Bolton went across the street
with the Reverend and a few other guys. There
was one other guy from our band and another guy
from their band, so there were four of five of those
guys. They went across to this place called Sudsy's,
which is a laundromat/bar/nightclub where they
have bands play.

There was this local band playing, and Reverend's
gang was getting kind of looped over there, having
some drinks and stuff. The Reverend was buying
everybody drinks, and Dan Bolton was listening to
the band; and decided it was about time they
finished. So he took it upon himself to jump right
into their drum set. The guys in the band got
really pissed-off at him, they kicked his ass,
punched him in the nose. He was bleeding all over
the place. It turned into a little bit of a brawl. So
they all leave and they go outside and they are all
sort of recombubulating, when Bolton remembers
that he still has a drink inside.

Meanwhile, while he, the Reverend and another
guy were outside; inside some girl was saying,
"Oh!! Those are the guys from the Supersuckers
and the Reverend Horton Heat, and they played
across the street and they're rich. And they're just

coming over here to mess up our good time!!!" She got a good twenty people on her side, thinking that we were some evil rich people for some reason, which couldn't be any further from the truth.

So Bolton goes back inside to get his drink. By this time the band had set back up and started playing again. But as soon as they saw him, they dropped all their instruments and kicked his ass again! Some guy was kicking him in the head, and Bolton was bleeding all over the place, and laughing because he couldn't believe they were so mad at him as to kick his ass twice. Then a big giant brawl broke out with the Reverend and their drummer, who is a really big guy, and everybody else in the place. The next day both Dan Bolton and the Reverend Horton Heat had huge black eyes, and our guitar player had a big bruise on his back where he got kicked or something like that. The whole time I was passed out in our van, and our drummer was doing this radio interview down the street. He was having a nightmare of his own, and he and our roadie ended up pissing all over the radio station. So it was a pretty good rock night all around. (September 1992) Eddie Spaghetti.

Surgery

"Then all of the sudden we hear this big 'BOOM!' and all the windows in the bar come flying in."

SURGERY

Interviewed by Gary at The Casbah, San Diego, CA.
The whole band was present.

A).....Last year, March......March 1991. We're in
Madison WI, we play O'Kayz Coral. We get pretty
fucked up, everybody's just like hanging out. We
had a good show, a lotta people, it was fun.

B) My mother was there, and like all of her friends
were there. 'Cause my mother lives near there.

A) All of a sudden, we're walking out, we're ready
to go out, load out the stuff. We load everything
into the van. Everyone's like, cool (we're done
loading gear). I drop our drummer's cymbal bag
and it goes "boom" all other the street. He wanted
to go in the van and smoke a joint and we were all
like, "Fag, the bars are closing...."

B) Andy was there and we were asking Andy if we
could get pot. And he was like, "No we can't get pot
this late." So we thought, "All right, lets go back
inside and get one more beer." So we're moving
back into the bar starting to take off our jackets,
but before we could even get to the bar - I mean
this is 30 seconds from walking out of our van - the
lights go out in the bar. We don't hear anything.
We hear no brakes screeching.....

A) Then all of a sudden we hear this big "BOOM!"
And all the windows in the bar come flying in. The
whole club goes black.

B) We were all just like, "What!?" (Stunned). I go
running outside, and like I'm freaking out, and I
see this truck and our van, this old van....

A) An 18-Wheeler has hit our van! With a full load!

B) It was a small street in Madison. Why an 18-Wheeler would even be in this part of town, off the highway.......

Sean: It came off the highway, crossed the median, smashed into a car in back of our van and killed a kid. Totally, like, you know, demolished this kid. This kid was mush.

B) I thought he was asleep in one of our sleeping bags you know, on the street. He was gone!

Sean: He was gone, he was gone, he was gone!

Gary: Was the kid in the other car?

B) No, this kid was like walking down the street with his girl friend and they were at a club up the street.

Sean: And the kid said: "Hey, there's a truck that's out of control." And the next thing you know, he was dead.

B) The girl was pulling her hair out. His girlfriend was pulling her hair out. Her head was bleeding.

Sean: The cops had to restrain her.

B) They put her in a straight jacket. I went outside and I looked and the first thing I see is this beautiful that I had fucking flying down the road, this three and a half ton '74 ambulance, flying down the road, with nobody in it. Just like demolished, like flying down the road. And there was this semi-truck there. My first thought – I'm wasted – I want to kill this guy in the semi-truck, but his door is locked and he's unconscious. So I'm picking up bricks and I'm whipping them at the window (of the truck), 'cause I want to kick the shit out of the guy, I'm gonna kill this mother fucker! And the next thing I know, I realized that the dude is dead.

Sean: He (B) was in real bad shock.

Gary: The truck driver was dead too?

Sean: No, not the guy in the truck, it was the kid walking down the street. The kid walking down the street was mush.

B) Telephone poles are still falling at this point. Sparks are flying.

Sean: Sparks are flying and gasoline and diesel fuel are spilling everywhere. So we were like sure that there was gonna be an explosion. Meanwhile, it's like, fucking 60 below, with the wind chill factor. And we were freezing. And our van is thrashed! Our van is totalled. And a guy is laying dead, his girlfriend is freaking out, pulling out her hair.......

B) Her head was bleeding! (from her pulling out her hair)

Sean:...the inside of the club is totally wrecked! All the windows came flying through. There are power lines down. My father called it "hyper-real." He said: "Was it hyper-real ?" And I said, "It was hyper-real!" So we go out, it was our bass player's van, and he's like pissed off. He wants to throw a brick and kill the guy who's been driving this truck.

B) We find out the next day that this guy had been unconscious for a half a mile, in a semi-truck, a fully loaded semi-truck for a half a mile. Knocking all this shit down and finally hits us. The guy's got a "White Aryan Cross" tattoo on one arm, a swastika tattoo on the other arm.

Sean: "Aryan Brotherhood" on one arm and ......

B) .....and a wooden leg! We find out a few months later he had been let out of prison a year before hand - he killed his father when he was 18 years

old and was in jail for 11 years. He was a "good ol'
boy from Mississippi."

Sean: Yeah, he lost his trucking license in Mississippi, but got it back in Louisiana. And the head-
line the next morning was - *I Guess I Was Pretty
Drunk.*

B) The guy had a blood-alcohol level of .27.

Sean: So instead of like beating his fucking head in
and killing him, we ended up pulling him out of
the truck and putting him in a fuckin' blanket so
that he wouldn't die. He went into shock. He had a
peg-leg too, half of his leg was gone.

B) A wooden leg, the guy had a fuckin' wooden leg,
man! It was nuts!

Sean: It was absolutely insane!

Gary: So you guys dragged him out of the truck?

Sean: Yeah.

B) Wait, wait, before I see the dead kid, I'm set on
killing this guy. Smashing his skull with a fucking
brick. And then we finally get him out of there, the
dudes eyes are way in the back of his head....He's
gone.

Gary: Did the cops show up?

B) The cops showed up like 20 minutes later!

Sean: We had him in a blanket, you know, we were
saving him even though we wanted to kill him. He
ruined our lives! He wrecked all of our equipment
and our van!

Sean and B together: His name was Cecil E.
Shempert!

Sean: He's doing 17 (years)! He's becoming a bride
in Jocko's Big House right now!

B) Yeah, he's doing a little helmet washing right

fucking now, man! Thank god, man! If I ever meet that guy again...........

Sean: So the headlines the next day - *I Guess I Was A Little Drunk* - Yeah, I guess you were dude. He killed a guy! And the guy was like a Phi Beta Kappa!

Gary: So what did you guys do?

Sean: We rented a van. All our equipment was trashed! Gone! Man!

B) We had to cancel the last three weeks of our tour......And the shit he was carrying in the back of his truck was like a full load of Pig Nose Pencil Holders.

Sean: He went to a bar, had a few pitchers and ruined our lives! And we're still fucking haggling with the insurance company. We have to go to court. They are all, "Well, were the instruments yours?" Of course they were ours!

Gary: You didn't get anything.....

B) Not yet, but we're gonna sue the fuck out of him! And now they (the courts) want to see our last work receipts, last jobs, IRS shit.

Sean: No one has any money! We're all fucking broke in this band! It's just fucking unbelievable.

UK Subs

"We saw him,
like, run off
the stage
holding his
bottom..."

UK SUBS

Brian (bass) and Matthew (drums), interviewed by Greg Jacobs at Pacific Shores Bar, San Diego, CA.

Brian: Well...what happened was, well, we were in Palm Beach, Florida and we were doing a show. Charlie, our singer, is like 48 (years old), he's like a continent. He fucking jumped up and he shit his pants on stage. And we went, "What is that smell? That is fucking horrible. What is it?" He tried to run off and then he just carried on (with the show). Four hours later he's like talking to the kids and everyone's going, (makes sniffing sounds) What's that smell? what, what is that smell?" (in a mock child's voice). And Charlie had crapped in his pants; our singer...he's too old.

Greg: So he crapped in his pants?

Brian: Yeah, he packed, he packed his pants.

Matthew: What happened was, like, we were play-ing a song, and we saw him run off the stage holding his bottom, yelling, "Oh NO NO NO NO NO." You've got to put that in there 'cos that's a fucking great quote from Charlie, you know.

Brian and Matthew: 'Cause Charlie says, " Oh no no no no no no no no no!" all the time.

Matthew: And like he came at us, after he finished the end of the song, and he told us that he crapped himself the next day, but, the whole thing about it was that he was hanging around for fucking about six hours talking to all these little kids with a pile of crap in his fucking underwear. And like signing autographs, you know (laughs).

Brian: What a cunt. (ALL LAUGH)

"The RV broke
down in the same
cornfield that
Buddy Holly died
in. Ooh cool!"

X / John Doe

Spoken by John Doe

X: In 1993, the Hey Zeus Record on Mercury Records.

During that tour which we started in July, our first of the East Coast, there was a heat wave that lasted for exactly 10 days. 10 days that X was on the East Coast, it was never below 90° maybe 92°. It was never below 90% humidity. But the heat wave fuckin' died – X played – X rocked the fuck out. Then we moved over to the Midwest where they had the great flood of 1993 and we played through the flood, through the waters, driving over the Mississippi many, many times. In St. Louis the waters were lapping the back door of Mississippi Nights. And from there, we continued on the National disaster tour of 1993.

John Doe:

In 1989, John Doe and his solo band had their RV vehicle break down in the cornfield that Buddy Holly died in. Ooh, Cool! The RV broke down in the same town that Buddy Holly, Richie Valens and the Big Bopper died back in the 50s. After almost getting arrested for using a credit card that was not in my name, we escaped miraculously and rented a truck. After having climbed in the equipment truck, which was a cube van rent-a-truck from Rider, we drove about 700 miles to Minneapolis, Minnesota to play at the 7th Street Entrance of the First Avenue Club. We arrived 5 minutes, or maybe 15 minutes before we were supposed to go on. The band walked downstairs to drink a bottle of tequila and went on stage, after having ridden about 10 hours in the dark in the back of a cube van. I guess that's rock 'n roll huh? Wow!